D0343392

Becoming a champion could not have been possible without the support of my parents and sister, the encouragement of my friends, classmates, and teachers, and the organization of the National Geographic Society's members and staff. They all helped me tremendously on my path to success, especially my mom, who constantly encouraged me, provided me with unwavering support, and her strong belief about my capability of becoming a champion.

# geography

THE ORGANIZED WAY TO PREPARE FOR THE NATIONAL GEOGRAPHIC BEE

australia and
oceania

## PRANAY VARADA

*Champion of the 29th National Geographic Bee*

# how to use this book

This book consists of fourteen profiles, one for each country of the Australian continent and Oceanian region. These profiles are a revised version of the ones I used to study with leading up to my victory in the 29th National Geographic Bee. Each profile consists of five sections: **Political Geography, Physical Geography, Economic Geography, Historical Geography, Cultural Geography,** and **Destinations.** In instances where the topic is a place, you will find an article describing the place and facts related to that place. Here is an example:

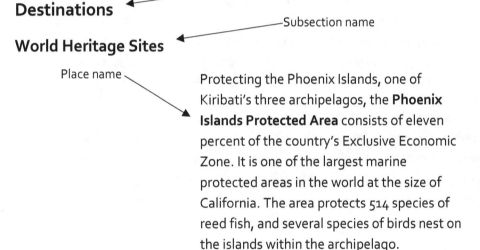

Section name

## Destinations

Subsection name

## World Heritage Sites

Place name

Protecting the Phoenix Islands, one of Kiribati's three archipelagos, the **Phoenix Islands Protected Area** consists of eleven percent of the country's Exclusive Economic Zone. It is one of the largest marine protected areas in the world at the size of California. The area protects 514 species of reed fish, and several species of birds nest on the islands within the archipelago.

While reading these profiles, you will notice that subsections differ between countries. If subsections are not present, it is because a) the subsection is not available (for example, Tuvalu has no rivers) or b) there is not sufficient information. Otherwise, each section contains all important and necessary facts you need to know to succeed in competition. If a country contains more than ten of a particular feature, only the ten most important features are mentioned (in most cases).

Some tips on how to use these profiles:

- **Put all of these places on a map.** Mapping will help you internalize the relative locations of places to each other and give you some perspective on what the country really looks like.
- **Read the profiles one country at a time.** If you read too many countries at once, it might lead you to mix up a fact from one country with another from a different country, which can be fatal in competition.
- **Quiz yourself.** The only way to make sure you know the answers on competition day is by making sure you know the answers beforehand. You can also combine information from profiles into a continent quiz, which allows you to have questions where a country and not a place is the answer. Remember, **the place name is the most important detail,** and memorizing the supporting facts can give you more evidence to choose one answer over another.

Remember, these profiles *can* also be read just for fun! If you happen to be traveling to one of the countries in this book, each profile does contain sections on national parks, tourist attractions, and UNESCO World Heritage Sites, which are often the defining features of a country. If you just want to know more about a country, this is also the place to find what you're looking for!

Good luck!

# table of contents

# australia and oceania

# australia and oceania

The smallest continent/region by area and the second smallest by population, **Australia and Oceania** consists of the main continent of Australia and, in general, the islands of the southern and western Pacific. The region consists of fourteen countries and sixteen territories owned by five different countries.

Australia is the largest of the countries by area and population (and the sixth largest country in the world), followed by Papua New Guinea and New Zealand. Sydney is the largest city. Apart from the main landmasses, Oceania contains three main subregions: Melanesia, Micronesia, and Polynesia. By some definitions, the western half of the island of New Guinea, which is Indonesian territory, is part of the region, as are Hawaii and Easter Island.

Christianity is the most practiced religion; English is the most spoken language. Nauru is the most densely populated country while Australia is the least densely populated.

The extreme points of Oceania:

- Northernmost point: Kure Atoll, United States
- Southernmost point: Jacquemart Island, New Zealand
- Westernmost point: Dirk Hartog Island, Australia
- Easternmost point: Easter Island, Chile (if Easter Island is included); Ducie Island, United Kingdom (not including Easter Island)

The extreme points of Australia (mainland):

- Northernmost point: Cape York Peninsula, Queensland
- Southernmost point: South Point, Wilsons Promontory, Victoria
- Easternmost point: Cape Byron, New South Wales
- Westernmost point: Steep Point, Western Australia

# australia

# australia

## Political Geography

**Sobriquet** Land Down Under

**Capital** Canberra

**Five Largest Provinces (Area)** Western Australia, Queensland, Northern Territory, South Australia, New South Wales

**Five Largest Provinces (Population)** New South Wales, Victoria, Queensland, Western Australia, South Australia

## Five Largest Cities

| City | State | Tourist Attractions | Body of Water |
|------|-------|---------------------|---------------|
| **Sydney** | New South Wales | Port Jackson, Sydney Opera House, Sydney Harbor Bridge, Bondi Beach, Darling Harbor, The Rocks, Taronga Zoo, Manly Beach, Sea Life Sydney Aquarium, Sydney Tower | Nepean River, Hawkesbury River, Parramatta River, Georges River, Cooks River, Sydney Harbor, Broken Bay, Botany Bay, Tasman Sea |

| City | State | Tourist Attractions | Body of Water |
|------|-------|---------------------|---------------|
| **Melbourne** | Victoria | Melbourne City Centre, Melbourne Zoo, Sea Life Melbourne Aquarium, Royal Botanic Gardens, National Gallery of Victoria, Queen Victoria Market, Yarra Valley, Melbourne Cricket Ground, Scienceworks, Old Melbourne Gaol | Yarra River, Port Phillip Bay |
| **Brisbane** | Queensland | Lone Pine Koala Sanctuary, Mount Coot-tha, Queensland Gallery of Modern Art, Roma Street Parkland, Mount Coot-tha Lookout, City Botanic Gardens, Suncorp Stadium, Wheel of Brisbane, Museum of Brisbane, South Bank Parklands | Brisbane River, Moreton Bay |

| City | State | Tourist Attractions | Body of Water |
|------|-------|--------------------|--------------|
| **Perth** | Western Australia | Kings Park, Swan Valley, Perth Zoo, Aquarium of Western Australia, Art Gallery of Western Australia, Hillarys Boat Harbor, Scitech, Western Australian Museum, Fremantle Prison, Adventure World | Canning River, Murray River, Serpentine River, Swan River, Indian Ocean |
| **Adelaide** | South Australia | Adelaide Zoo, Adelaide Botanic Garden, Art Gallery of South Australia, South Australian Museum, Cleland Conservation Park, Adelaide Oval, Botanic Park, Migration Museum, Mount Lofty, Victoria Square | Gulf Saint Vincent |

# Physical Geography

**Relative Size** About the size of the contiguous United States minus Kansas or twice the size of Argentina

**Highest Point** Located in the Snowy Mountains in the Kosciuszko National Park of New South Wales, Mount Kosciuszko is the highest point of Australia at 7,310 feet above sea level. It is next to Mount Townsend, the second highest point of the continent. Although the peak is the highest on the Australian continent, Mawson Peak on Heard Island and Mount Menzies, Mount McClintock, and Dome Argus in the Australian Antarctic Territory are all higher than it. The nearby Lake Cootapatamba is the highest lake in the country.

**Lowest Point** Known to the indigenous people of the region as Kati Thanda, **Lake Eyre** contains the lowest natural point in Australia at 49 feet below sea level. On the rare occasions that it fills, it is the largest lake in the country and the eighteenth largest in the world. The endorheic lake is 435 miles north of Adelaide and is fed by the Warburton River. Sometimes the algae *Dunaliella salina* causes the lake to take on a pink hue.

## Deserts

The largest desert in Australia, the **Great Victoria Desert** consists of many small sand hills, grassland plains, desert pavement areas, and salt lakes. The Nullarbor Plain to the south separates it from the Indian Ocean. This region of the country has the most populous and most healthy indigenous population. Only a few species of flora and fauna can survive in the sparsely populated and extremely arid region.

Located in northwestern Western Australia, the **Great Sandy Desert** is the second largest desert in Australia. It lies north of the Gibson Desert and west of the Tanami Desert. The desert contains large ergs and Wolfe Creek, a well-known meteorite impact site. The region is sparsely populated and the population is mainly Aboriginal. Rainfall is high by desert standards although summer temperatures are some of the hottest in the country. The desert contains gold and uranium deposits and *Triodia* grass. It was first crossed by

British explorer Peter Warburton, who walked from central Australia to the Western Australian coast.

Located mainly in the Northern Territory with a small portion in Western Australia, the **Tanami Desert** was the Northern Territory's final frontier. It has a rocky terrain and small hills. Several of Australia's rare and endangered species can be found in the desert. It is crossed by the Tanami Road, which connects Halls Creek in Western Australia to Alice Springs in the Northern Territory.

The fourth largest desert in Australia, the **Simpson Desert** is the world's largest sand dune desert. It is part of the Great Artesian Basin and the Lake Eyre basin, one of the largest inland drainage areas in the world. Although no maintained roads cross the desert, it is still popular with tourists in winter. Water from the basin rises to the surface at many natural springs including Dalhousie Springs.

Located in Western Australia, the **Gibson Desert** is in an almost pristine state. A group of the Pintupi people who were living in the desert are believed to have been the last uncontacted tribe in Australia. The desert lies between Lake Disappointment and Lake Macdonald along the Tropic of Capricorn, north of the Great Sandy Desert but south of the Great Victoria Desert.

## Basins

The largest and deepest artesian aquifer in the world, the **Great Artesian Basin** provides the only reliable source of freshwater in a large portion of inland Australia. It lies under 23% of the continent, including the Northern Territory, Queensland, New South Wales, and South Australia. The basin is estimated to contain 15,600 cubic miles of groundwater.

## Plateaus

Located in the Great Dividing Range in New South Wales, the **Dorrigo Plateau** is located 360 miles north of Sydney. The highest point is Barren Mountain. The plateau is surrounded by Guy Fawkes River National Park.

Part of the northern Flinders Ranges, the **Mawson Plateau** is located in South Australia. It is located within the arid region surrounding Lake Eyre. The plateau is a granite batholith, or large emplacement of igneous intrusive rock.

## Mountain Ranges

Australia's most substantial mountain range and the third longest terrestrial mountain range in the world, the **Great Dividing Range** runs 2,175 miles from Dauan Island off the northeastern tip of Queensland to Grampians National Park in southwestern Victoria. Mount Kosciuszko, the highest point of Australia, is also the highest point of the mountain range. The highest areas of the range, in southern New South Wales and eastern Victoria, are known as the Australian Alps. The central area of the mountain range has hundreds of peaks with canyons, valleys, and plains. Many spectacular waterfalls can be found in the Australian Alps. Canberra, the Australian capital, is located in the upland area of the range. 45 national parks can be found in the range.

## Mountain Passes

Located in the Great Dividing Range in Queensland, the **Cunninghams Gap** is the major route over the Scenic Rim, a forested area of the range. It is located in Main Range National Park and contains part of the Cunningham Highway, which connects the Darling Downs and the Fassifern Valley.

## Valleys

Located 37 miles northeast of Adelaide, the **Barossa Valley** is formed by the North Para River. It is a notable wine-producing region and tourist destination. The valley is known primarily for its red wine, including an ingredient in Penfolds Grange, Australia's most famous wine. Agriculture is also significant in the valley's economy.

Located in New South Wales 75 to 193 miles north of Sydney, the **Hunter Region** contains the Hunter River and its tributaries. It is known mostly for its wineries and coal industry. Newcastle is the largest city of the region. Many national parks can be found in the area, which is also a good place for wine production due to its proximity to Sydney. The Pokolbin area is the center of the wine country.

## Islands

The largest island of Australia, **Tasmania** is separated from southeastern Australia by the Bass Strait, which is 150 miles wide. It is a state of the country, with its capital and largest city at Hobart. The island is located in the path of the "Roaring Forties" wind. It has many jagged peaks resulting from recent glaciation and is the most mountainous state in the country. Many vineyards are scattered across the island. It is promoted as a natural state, with 45% of the island being protected. 334 other islands surround it.

Located with of the Cobourg Peninsula north of Darwin, **Melville Island** is located in the Timor Sea and is the second largest island of Australia. Together with Bathurst Island, Melville Island forms the Tiwi Islands.

The third largest island in Australia, **Kangaroo Island** is located in South Australia seventy miles southwest of Adelaide and eight miles from the Fleurieu Peninsula. The island is separated from Yorke Peninsula to the northwest by the Investigator Strait and from the Fleurieu Peninsula to the northeast by the Backstairs Passage. Kingscote is the largest settlement on the island, which is noted for its honey. Its Ligurian honey bees form the world's only pure-bred and disease-free population of this type of bee. The island is one of the state's most popular tourist attractions. Flinders Chase

National Park on the western end of the island is the best known nature reserve.

The largest island in the Gulf of Carpentaria, **Groote Eylandt** lies 31 miles from the mainland of the Northern Territory and 391 miles from Darwin. It is owned by the Anindilyakwa people, for which it is their homeland. The settlement of Angurugu contains most of the island's population. The island is generally quite low-lying.

One of the two Tiwi Islands along with Melville Island, **Bathurst Island** is located in the Timor Sea and lies 43 miles north of Darwin. The settlement of Wurrumiyanga contains most of the island's population.

**Fraser Island** (see World Heritage Sites)

Located in Bass Strait, **Flinders Island** is the largest island in the Furneaux Group. It is located on 40 degrees south and has a large mountainous area. The coastal areas are mostly covered in scrub and shrubs.

Located in the "Roaring Forties" of the Bass Strait, halfway between Tasmania and Victoria, **King Island** has Currie as its largest town and administrative center. It is surrounded by three smaller islands.

The northernmost of the 22 islands of the Wellesley Islands, **Mornington Island** is located in the Gulf of Carpentaria. The majority of the islanders are Aboriginal and the largest settlement in Gununa.

## Archipelagos

Located off the coast of Western Australia in the Kimberley Region, the **Bonaparte Archipelago** lies between Collier Bay to the southwest and the Admiralty Gulf to the northeast. The largest island in the group is Augustus Island.

Located off the coast of Western Australia in the Kimberley Region, the **Buccaneer Archipelago** is located at the head of King Sound. The island's rocks are over two billion years old and has its largest island as Koolan Island.

Located at the eastern end of the Bass Strait between the state of Victoria on the mainland and the island of Tasmania, the **Furneaux Group** contains Flinders Island, one of Australia's largest islands. Whitemark, a settlement on this island, is the administrative center of the area.

Located off the western coast of the Eyre Peninsula in South Australia, the **Investigator Group** lies at the end of the Great Australian Bight. Flinders Island (not the one northeast of Tasmania) is the largest island of the group. The five island groups of the archipelago are the Waldegrave Islands, The Watchers, the Topgallant Islands, the Ward Islands, and the Pearson Isles.

Located twelve miles north of Barrow Island and 81 miles off the Pilbara coast of northwestern Australia, the **Montebello Islands** were the site of three British nuclear tests, one in 1952 and two in 1956. The islands support over one percent of the world populations of fairy terns, roseate terns, and sooty oystercatchers. The climate is hot and arid.

Located at the eastern end of the Great Australian Bight and off the northwestern coast of the Eyre Peninsula, the **Nuyts Archipelago** is biologically unique in South Australia due to the influence of the Leeuwin Current. Saint Peter Island is the largest island of the archipelago and is also the most accessible island. The islands support over one percent of the world populations of short-tailed shearwaters, white-faced storm petrels, and pied oystercatchers.

Located off the southern coast of Western Australia, the **Recherche Archipelago** has Middle Island as its largest island. Only Woody Island allows tourists to enter. Recreational and commercial fishing are the main activities in the archipelago. The area is a biodiversity hotspot with populations of terrestrial flora and fauna, some unique to the archipelago. The islands support over one percent of the world populations of flesh-footed shearwaters, sooty oystercatchers, fairy terns, and white-faced storm petrels.

Located in the Spencer Gulf twelve miles off the eastern coast of the Eyre Peninsula in South Australia, the **Sir Joseph Banks Group** is considered to be an important seabird breeding site. Splisby Island is privately owned and is grazed by sheep. The islands contain over one percent of the world populations of white-faced storm petrels, Cape Barren geese, black-faced cormorants, and Pacific gulls.

Located in Torres Strait, which separates the Cape York Peninsula of far northern Australia from the island of New Guinea, the **Torres Strait Islands** are mostly part of Queensland, although a few islands close to the New Guinean coast are part of the Western Province of Papua New Guinea. Torres Strait Islanders are the indigenous peoples of the islands are distinct from other Aboriginal peoples of Australia. The islands are threatened by rising sea levels, although no relocation strategies have been put in place.

**Whitsunday Islands** (see Tourist Attractions)

## Rivers

| River | Source | Mouth | Cities (if any) |
|---|---|---|---|
| **Murray** | Cowombat Flat (North South Wales-Victoria border) | Indian Ocean (South Australia) | Albury (New South Wales), Wodonga, Echuca, Swan Hill, Mildura (Victoria), Renmark, Murray Bridge (South Australia) |
| **Murrumbidgee** | Peppercorn Hill (New | Murray River (New South | Cooma, Canberra, Gundagai, Wagga |

| River | Source | Mouth | Cities (if any) |
|-------|--------|-------|-----------------|
| | South Wales) | Wales-Victoria border) | Wagga, Narrandera, Hay, Balranald (New South Wales) |
| Darling | Confluence of the Barwon and Culgoa Rivers (New South Wales) | Murray River (New South Wales-Victoria border) | Bourke, Wilcannia, Menindee, Wentworth (New South Wales) |
| Lachlan | Great Dividing Range (New South Wales) | Great Cumbung Swamp (New South Wales) | Bevendale, Breadalbane, Reids Flat, Wyangala, Cowra, Gooloogong, Forbes, Euabalong, Condobolin, Lake Cargelligo, Hillston, Booligal, O`xley (New South Wales) |
| Warrego | Mount Ka Ka Mundi (Queensland) | Darling River (New South Wales) | Augathella, Charleville, Wyandra, Cunnamulla (Queensland) |

## Lakes

A large endorheic lake in central South Australia, **Lake Gairdner** is the third largest salt lake in Australia when it is flooded. It is west of Lake Torrens and is part of Lake Gairdner National Park.

Located at the southern edge of the Little Sandy Desert, **Lake Carnegie** is a large ephemeral lake in Western Australia. It lies to the north of the main goldfields region of the state. The lake fills only during rare periods of significant rainfall.

**Lake Eyre** (see Lowest Point)

The largest of the ephemeral salt lakes in Western Australia and the Northern Territory, **Lake Mackay** is the largest lake in Western Australia. The lake bed is extremely arid and salts and other minerals are carried to the surface through capillary action caused by evaporation.

An ephemeral salt lake in central South Australia, **Lake Torrens** is located within Lake Torrens National Park. It lies between the Arcoona Plateau to the west and the Flinders Ranges to the east 214 miles north of Adelaide.

The westernmost lake in Australia, **Lake Macleod** is influenced by the Western Australian Current. The lake area supports over one percent of the world populations of red-necked stints, curlew sandpipers, banded stilts, red-necked avocets, red-capped plovers, and dusky gerygones.

A large endorheic lake in South Australia, **Lake Frome** lies mostly below sea level. The area surrounding the lake has little rainfall and is sparsely settled. Two significant uranium deposits lie near the lake, which lies east of the northern Flinders Ranges.

Located in the southwestern corner of the Northern Territory, **Lake Amadeus** contains over 600 million tons of salt. It is the largest salt lake in the Northern Territory and is usually a dry crust of salt.

## Bays

A large open bay off the central and western portions of the southern coastline of Australia, the **Great Australian Bight** borders the states of South Australia, Tasmania, Victoria, and Western Australia. It empties into the Indian Ocean and borders the Nullarbor Plain on the mainland. The coastline is mainly made up of cliff faces up to 200 feet high. The waters of the bight are high in biodiversity, especially in zooplankton. Bluefin tuna are commonly fished for in the bight.

Located in southern New South Wales, **Jervis Bay** is said to possess the whitest sand in the world. An area of land next to the bay is known as the Jervis Bay Territory, administered as if it was part of the Australian Capital Territory. This territory's purpose is to give Canberra access to the sea. The bay is a drowned river valley that empties into the Tasman Sea. Booderee National Park, Jervis Bay National Park, and Jervis Bay Marine Park protect the bay, which is well known for recreational fishing and scuba diving. Humpback whales migrate across the eastern coast from June to November. Tourism is an important source of income for the local economy.

## Gulfs

A large, shallow sea enclosed on three sides by northern Australia and on one side by the Arafura Sea, the **Gulf of Carpentaria** borders Arnhem Land in the Northern Territory and the Cape York Peninsula in Queensland. Groote Eylandt is the largest island in the gulf. The Great Dividing Range parallels the entire eastern and southeastern coast. Commercial shrimp operations take place in the gulf.

A large inlet of water in South Australia, **Gulf Saint Vincent** is bordered by the Yorke Peninsula to the west and the mainland and the Fleurieu Peninsula to the east. Adelaide, the South Australian capital, lies halfway along the eastern coast.

The westernmost of two large inlets on the South Australian coast, **Spencer Gulf** is bordered by the Eyre Peninsula to the west and the Yorke Peninsula to the east. The Yorke Peninsula separates it from the smaller Gulf Saint Vincent. Many of South Australia's iconic marine species can be found in the gulf.

## Seas

Located north of the Gulf of Carpentaria, east of the Timor Sea, southeast of the Banda and Ceram Seas, south of New Guinea, and west of the Torres Strait which connects it to the Coral Sea, the **Arafura Sea** is bordered by Australia, Indonesia, and Papua New Guinea. It is home to one of the richest marine fisheries in the world and has a lot of potential in terms of exports.

Bordered by Australia, New Caledonia (France), Papua New Guinea, the Solomon Islands, and Vanuatu, the **Coral Sea** contains the world's largest reef system, the Great Barrier Reef (a UNESCO World Heritage Site). It is a popular tourist attraction for birds and aquatic life. It borders the Solomon Sea to the north, the Pacific Ocean to the east, Queensland to the west, the Tasman Sea to the south, and the Torres Strait (which connects it to the Arafura Sea) in the northwest.

Named after the Dutch explorer Abel Janszoon Tasman, the first European to encounter Tasmania and New Zealand, the **Tasman Sea** is situated between southeastern Australia and New Zealand. It is informally referred to by Australians and New Zealanders as "The Ditch". Lord Howe and Norfolk Islands, both part of Australia, are the major islands in the sea. Auckland, Newcastle, Sydney, Wellington, and Wollongong are the major cities on the sea.

A relatively shallow sea south of the island of Timor, west of the Arafura Sea, north of Australia, and east of the Indian Ocean, the **Timor Sea** contains many reefs, uninhabited islands, and hydrocarbon reserves. Darwin, the capital of the Northern Territory, lies on the gulf. The Joseph Bonaparte,

Beagle, and Van Diemen Gulfs in Australia are inlets of the sea. It was the location of Australia's largest oil spill, the Montara oil spill, which leaked out 400 barrels of oil each day in 2009. The sea was also the site of the Battle of Timor in World War II between the Allied forces of Australia, the Netherlands, the United Kingdom, the United States, Portugal, and Timor and the Axis power of Japan.

## Straits

Separating the island of Tasmania, the largest in Australia, from the Australian mainland state of Victoria, the **Bass Strait** contains many islands, including King Island and Flinders Island. In the early 19th century, the strait was a safer and shorter route for ships going from Europe and India to Sydney despite its difficult waters.

Located between the Western Province of Papua New Guinea and Australia's Cape York Peninsula in Queensland, the **Torres Strait** is 93 miles wide at its narrowest width. It links the Arafura Sea in the west to the Coral Sea in the east. The Endeavour Strait separates Prince of Wales (Muralug) Island and mainland Australia. The strait allows illegal immigrants from Papua New Guinea to enter Australia.

## Isthmuses

A narrow isthmus between the Tasman Peninsula and mainland Tasmania, **Eaglehawk Neck** is a well-known holiday destination. It forms a natural gateway to the peninsula, which was used by the British in the 1830s when a line of dogs were chained to posts to prevent convicts from escaping Port Arthur.

Connecting North Bruny and South Bruny, the two parts of Bruny Island, **The Neck** is an important breeding site for short-tailed shearwaters and fairy penguins. It is located between Great Bay to the northwest and Adventure

Bay to the southeast. Bruny Island is separated from Tasmania by the D'Entrecasteaux Channel and borders Storm Bay to the northeast.

## Peninsulas

One of the last remaining wilderness areas on the planet, the **Cape York Peninsula** is located in far northern Queensland. It is the largest unspoiled wilderness in northern Australia, bordered by the Gulf of Carpentaria to the west, the Coral Sea to the east, and the Torres Strait to the north. Its backbone is the Great Dividing Range, and the climate is tropical and monsoonal. The peninsula's rivers are important for replenishing the Great Artesian Basin. Over 1,000 plant species and 700 vertebrate land animal species can be found in the region. Cooktown, in the southeast, is the administrative and commercial center, while Weipa, on the Gulf of Carpentaria, is the largest settlement.

Located 217 miles east of Darwin in the Northern Territory, the **Cobourg Peninsula** is part of Garig Gunak Barlu National Park. It is separated from Croker Island in the east by the Bowen Strait and Melville Island in the west by the Dundas Strait. The Arafura Sea is to the north while the Van Diemen Gulf is to the south. The peninsula is a tourist attraction home to the world's largest herd of pure-strain banteng and a renowned Aboriginal culture.

A triangular peninsula in South Australia, the **Eyre Peninsula** is bounded on the east by the Spencer Gulf and on the west by the Great Australian Bight. The peninsula's main townships are Port Lincoln, Whyalla, Port Augusta, and Ceduna. The Gawler Ranges lie to the north.

Located in southeastern Tasmania, the **Tasman Peninsula** is connected to the Forestier Peninsula in the north by Eaglehawk Neck. It is surrounded by Norfolk Bay to the north, Frederick Henry Bay to the northwest, Storm Bay to the west and south, and the Tasman Sea to the east. The peninsula is home to the Port Arthur World Heritage Site, the top tourist attraction in the state.

Located northwest and west of Adelaide, the capital of South Australia, the **Yorke Peninsula** lies between Spencer Gulf in the west and Gulf Saint Vincent in the east. It is separated from Kangaroo Island to the south by the Investigator Strait. The peninsula is a major producer of grain, and its most populous town is Kadina. Its southwestern tip is home to Innes National Park.

## Capes

The easternmost point of the Australian mainland, **Cape Byron** lies two miles east of Byron Bay, projecting into the Pacific Ocean. The Cape Byron Light is Australia's most powerful lighthouse, dating back to 1901.

## Economic Geography

**Currency** Australian dollar

**Natural Resources** Rutile, zircon, bauxite, iron ore, ilmenite, alumina, gold, lithium, manganese ore, lead, zinc, uranium, silver, nickel, coal, natural gas, petroleum

**Agricultural Products** Cattle, calves, wheat, milk, fruit, nuts, vegetables, wool, barley, poultry, lambs, sugar cane

**Major Producer** Coal (fourth), uranium (third), thorium (second), aluminum (seventh), bauxite (first), copper (sixth), gold (second), iron ore (second), lithium (first), manganese (third), silver (fourth), tin (seventh), titanium (first), zinc (second), oats (fifth), chickpeas (second), pulses (fifth), beef (fifth), sheep (second), nuts (second), wool (second)

**Ports** Adelaide, Fremantle, Portland, Port Hedland (largest port), Port Lincoln, Port Pirie, Geelong, Melbourne, Darwin, Weipa, Bundaberg, Brisbane, Gladstone, Hay Point, Townsville, Botany Bay (Port Botany), Hobart, Newcastle, Port Jackson (Sydney), Port Kembla

## Historical Geography

**Former Name** New Holland

**Former Capital** Melbourne (*de facto*, 1901-1927)

**Historic Cities** Sydney (est. 1788), Paramatta (est. 1788), Hobart (est. 1803), Newcastle (est. 1804), Launceston (est. 1806)

**Empires** Dutch Empire (named the continent "New Holland"), British Empire (claimed New South Wales in 1770)

**Natives** Aborigines

**Independence** From the United Kingdom, 1901

## Cultural Geography

**Language** None (official), English (national)

**Major Ethnic Groups** Some of these are mixed: English (36.1%), Australian (35.4%), Irish (10.4%), Scottish (8.9%), Italian (4.6%), German (4.5%), Chinese (4.3%), Indian (2%), Greek (1.9%), Dutch (1.7%)

**Religion** Roman Catholic (25.3%), Anglican (17.1%), other Christian (18.7%), Buddhist (2.5%), Muslim (2.2%), Hindu (1.3%), Jewish (0.5%), irreligious (22.3%), other (10.1%)

**Foods** Vegemite, macadamia nuts, Violet Crumble, Cherry Ripe, jaffa, Chiko Roll, dim sim, Tim Tam, fairy bread, lamington, Australian hamburger, Anzac biscuit, pavlova, meat pie, pie floater

# Destinations

## National Parks

Located 62 miles southwest of Darwin in the Northern Territory, **Litchfield National Park** was established in 1986 and attracts over 260,000 visitors each year. Aboriginal people have lived in the area for thousands of years. Wangi Falls is the most popular attraction due to it being easily accessible. The park offers a wide range of walking tracks and contains rich woodland flora communities with many different species of Australian fauna. The park is closer to Darwin than Kakadu National Park, making it more easily accessible.

Located in far northern Queensland, 933 miles north of Brisbane, **Daintree National Park** is part of the Wet Tropics of Queensland World Heritage Site. Most of the national park is covered by tropical rainforest, which could be the oldest existing rainforest in the world. The park contains significant populations of the cassowary, an endangered, flightless bird. Over 430 species of bird live in the park.

**Blue Mountains National Park** (see Tourist Attractions)

**Kakadu National Park** (see World Heritage Sites)

Located on Tasmania's eastern coast 78 miles northeast of Hobart, **Freycinet National Park** occupies a large portion of the Freycinet Peninsula. It is Tasmania's oldest national park along with Mount Field National Park. The secluded Wineglass Bay has been voted as one of the world's ten best beaches. The Hazards are a granite mountain range on the coast, positioned between Coles Bay and Wineglass Bay.

Located in southeastern New South Wales, **Kosciuszko National Park** has an alpine climate and the town of Cabramurra, the highest town in Australia. It is situated 220 miles south of Sydney and borders Alpine National Park in Victoria and Namagdi National Park in the Australian Capital Territory. The

Snowy, Murray, and Gungarlin Rivers all have their sources in the park. Mount Kosciuszko, the highest point on the Australian continent, is located in the park, as is Mount Townsend, the second highest point. Lake Cootapatamba is the highest lake in Australia. The Australian Alps Walking Track offers views of the peaks and the wilderness, popular with bushwalkers. Skiing is possible in the park.

Located in southwestern Victoria, **Port Campbell National Park** is located 120 miles southwest of Melbourne. It is located adjacent to Great Otway National Park and Bay of Islands Coastal Park. It is part of the Shipwreck Coast and contains several tourist geological tourist attractions. Many species of bird live in the park.

**Great Sandy National Park** (see Fraser Island World Heritage Site)

Located in the Central Highlands area of Tasmania, **Cradle Mountain-Lake Saint Clair National Park** is part of the Tasmanian Wilderness World Heritage Site. Forty to fifty-five percent of the park's alpine flora is endemic, while 68 percent of Tasmania's alpine rainforest species can be found in the park. Fungi form a large part of the park's biodiversity. The Overland Track is one of Australia's most famous bush treks, running from Cradle Mountain to Lake Saint Clair. Mount Ossa, the highest point of Tasmania, is located in the park. Cradle Mountain is a major tourist site in Tasmania due to its natural beauty while Lake Saint Clair is Australia's deepest lake.

**Uluṟu-Kata Tjuṯa National Park** (see World Heritage Sites)

## Tourist Attractions

A fourteen-mile stretch of beach near Broome in Western Australia, **Cable Beach** was named after the telegraph cable laid between Broome and Java in 1889. It is known for its white sands, beautiful sunsets, and blue waters. Camel rides are also possible on the beach.

**Fraser Island** (see World Heritage Sites)

A 151-mile stretch of road along the southeastern coast of Australia between the Victorian cities of Torquay and Allansford, the **Great Ocean Road** is the world's largest war memorial, built by soldiers returned from World War I between 1919 and 1932. It is one of the world's great scenic roads and runs right along the coastline. The Twelve Apostles, a collection of limestone stacks off the shore of Port Campbell National Park, are visible from the road. Despite their name, there are only eight apostles left. The stacks could be further eroded by the powerful waves.

Located in the East Kimberley region of Western Australia, **Purnululu National Park** is a UNESCO World Heritage Site that contains the Bungle Bungle Range's iconic sandstone domes, unusual and visually striking with their alternating orange and grey bands. The range is one of the most extensive and impressive sandstone karst terrain in the world. The park is 190 miles south of Kununurra, the largest town in Western Australia north of Broome.

Located in the Blue Mountains region of New South Wales, **Blue Mountains National Park** is located fifty miles west of Sydney. It is part of the Greater Blue Mountains Area World Heritage Site and the Great Dividing Range. Lake Burragorang, just outside the park, is the site of Warragamba Dam, the main source of drinking water for Sydney. Mount Werong is the highest point of the park, which is an uplifted plateau dissected by many rivers. The largest Australian carnivorous species in the park in the tiger quoll, mainland Australia's largest and the world's longest living carnivorous marsupial. The park is one of the most popular in Australia for hiking, canyoning, abseiling, rock climbing, and mountain biking. The Three Sisters, a major rock formation on the north escarpment of the Jamison Valley, is one of the Blue Mountains' most popular sites.

Located off the eastern Queensland coast, the **Whitsunday Islands** lies 560 miles north of Brisbane. Whitsunday Island is the largest island, although

Hamilton Island is the commercial center. The islands are one of the most popular yachting destinations in the Southern Hemisphere and are a popular tourist destination for travelers to Queensland and the Great Barrier Reef.

**Kakadu National Park** (see World Heritage Sites)

**Uluru** (see Uluru-Kata Tjuta National Park World Heritage Site)

**Great Barrier Reef** (see World Heritage Sites)

A multi-venue performing arts center in Sydney, the **Sydney Opera House** is situated on Bennelong Point in Sydney Harbor near the Sydney Harbor Bridge. It is adjacent to the Sydney central business district and the Royal Botanic gardens. The building has been identified as one of the 20th century's most distinctive buildings and is one of the most famous performing arts centers in the world. It is a UNESCO World Heritage Site for its modern expressionist design of large precast concrete shells. The Sydney Opera House Grand Organ is the largest mechanical tracker action organ in the world with over 10,000 pipes.

## World Heritage Sites

Located within the Alligator Rivers region of the Northern Territory 106 miles southeast of Darwin, **Kakadu National Park** is the largest national park in Australia. It is the size of Slovenia and contains the Ranger Uranium Mine, one of the most productive uranium mines in the world. The park is known for its great natural formations and its many Aboriginal cultural sites. Many species of flora and fauna can be found in the park, including one-third of Australia's bird species. The park's flora is among the richest in Northern Australia with over 1,700 plant species. The park is considered to be one of the most weed-free national parks in the world. The art sites of Ubirr, Burrunguy, and Nanguluwur are internationally recognized as outstanding examples of Aboriginal rock art. The park is a major tourist attraction in northern Australia for its many beautiful waterfalls including Gunlom Falls, Twin Falls, and Jim Jim Falls. Saltwater crocodiles can be found in the park.

The location of a world-renowned sandstone monolith, Uluru, which is 1,141 feet tall, **Uluru-Kata Tjuta National Park** is located in the southwestern Northern Territory. It is located 889 miles south of Darwin and 270 miles southwest of Alice Springs by road. Uluru, also known as Ayers Rock, is sacred to the Anangu, the Aboriginal people of the area. The formation is an inselberg of coarse-grained arkose, a type of sandstone, and conglomerate. It bears various inscriptions made by ancestral indigenous peoples. Kata Tjuta, also known as Mount Olga, is a group of large domed rock formations sixteen miles west of Uluru. There are many Pitjantjatjara legends associated with Uluru and Kata Tjuta. The area supports some of the most unusual flora and fauna on the planet. Over 400,000 visitors visit the park each year, and although the Anangu, the owners of the park, do not climb Uluru, tourists can still climb the formation.

The most extensive area of subtropical rainforest in the world, the **Gondwana Rainforests** contain fifty separate reserves from Newcastle to Brisbane around the New South Wales-Queensland border. The rainforest reserves are important for conservation due to their large amounts of rare or threatened plant and animal species. Main Range, Lamington, Mount Chinghee, Springbrook, Mount Barney, Barrington Tops, Dorrigo, Mount Warning, New England, Mebbin, Nightcap, Border Ranges, Oxley Wild Rivers, Washpool, Willi Willi, and Werrikimbe National Parks are all part of the site. Dorrigo and Springbrook National Parks are the most heavily visited sections of the site. The forests are named so due to its consistency of species since the former supercontinent of Gondwana existed.

Located along the southern coast of Queensland 120 miles north of Brisbane, **Fraser Island** is considered to be the largest sand island in the world. It is the largest island of Queensland and the largest island on the east coast of Australia. It is part of Great Sandy National Park and is a popular tourist destination. The Great Sandy Strait separates the island from the mainland. The sand is 98 percent quartz, and the eastern coast of the island is losing sand through erosion. The island has the second highest concentration of lakes in Australia after Tasmania. Lake Boomanjin is the largest perched lake in the world. The dingoes of the island are some of the last remaining pure dingoes in Eastern Australia and are prevented from being bred with other species. The eastern ground parrot, already extinct in parts of Australia, is still found on the island. The island is the only place on the planet where tall rainforest grows in sand. 350,000 to 500,000 visitors visit the island each year.

The world's largest coral reef, system, the **Great Barrier Reef** is composed of over 2,900 individual reefs and 900 islands stretching for over 1,400 miles in the Coral Sea off the coast of Queensland. It is the world's largest single structure made by living organisms, specifically coral polyps, and it is visible from outer space. The reef is a popular destination for tourists, especially in the Whitsunday Islands and Cairns regions. Tourism generates over $3 billion each year. Bramble Cay, the northernmost island, is located at the northeastern edge of the Torres Strait, while Lady Elliot Island, the southernmost island, is located near Fraser Island. The reef supports a wide variety of marine life, including many vulnerable or endangered species, some of them endemic. Thirty species of whales, dolphins, and porpoises live in the reef, as do over 1,500 fish species, seventeen species of sea snake, and six species of sea turtles. Saltwater crocodiles live in mangrove and salt marshes on the coast while 215 species of birds visit the reef or nest or roost on the islands. Climate change, pollution, crown-of-thorns starfish, and fishing threaten the health of the reef system. The Great Barrier Reef Marine Park protects a large portion of the reef from damaging activities. Due to its vast biodiversity, warm clear waters, and accessibility from tourist boats, the reef is a popular tourist destination, especially for scuba divers. Several of the islands are now tourist resorts.

Located along Queensland's northeastern portion of the Great Dividing Range, the **Wet Tropics of Queensland** have the highest concentration of primitive flowering plant families in the world. Only Madagascar and New Caledonia are comparable in plant endemism. The site stretches from Townsville to Cooktown, running parallel to the Great Barrier Reef, another World Heritage Site. Fifteen percent of the site includes Barron Gorge, Black Mountain (Kalkajaka), Cedar Bay, Daintree, Edmund Kennedy, Girringun, Kirrama, Kuranda, and Wooroonooran National Parks. Over 390 rare plant species can be found in the region, 74 of which are threatened. 85 plant species are endemic to the area, and there are more species of mangrove than anywhere else in Australia. The rare *Stockwellia quadrifida* trees only grow in small portions of the area. 65 percent of Australia's fern species can be found in the area, as can 370 species of bird, eleven of which are found nowhere else. The endangered southern cassowary and rare tiger quoll are some of the many threatened species, including Australia's rarest mammal, the tube-nosed insectivorous murina florious bat. A quarter of the country's rodent species are also found in the region. The expansion of the sugarcane industry poses a significant threat to some of the area's endangered ecosystems. The site is notable for meeting all four of UNESCO's criteria for selection as a natural heritage site.

One of the largest conservation areas in Australia, covering almost a fifth of Tasmania, the **Tasmanian Wilderness** is one of the last expanses of temperate wilderness in the world. The Southwestern Wilderness, which is included in the site, is a remote and inaccessible region of southwestern Tasmania consisting of untouched scenery, rugged peaks, wild rivers, unique flora and fauna, and a long, indented coastline. Southwest National Park is Tasmania's largest national park. Cradle Mountain-Lake Saint Clair, Franklin-Gordon Wild Rivers, Hartz Mountains, Mole Creek Karst, Walls of Jerusalem, and Mount Field National Parks are also part of the site. The rivers are rich with fish, while a small portion of the site is home to the summer breeding grounds of the highly endangered orange-bellied parrot. The area's weather is varied during the year due to its location in the Roaring Forties. The site is notable for being one of the only two World Heritage Sites that meet seven of

UNESCO's ten criteria for selection as a site, the other being Mount Tai in China.

Located about 500 miles north of Perth in one of the westernmost regions of Australia, **Shark Bay** was the country's first World Heritage Site. 190 miles of limestone cliffs overlook the bay, which is an area of major zoological important. It is home to about 10,000 dugongs, around 12.5 percent of the world population. There are 26 threatened mammal species, over 230 species of bird, nearly 150 species of reptile, and over 320 fish species. The whale shark, the world's largest fish, gathers in the bay during full moons in April and May. The Wooramel Seagrass Bank is the largest seagrass bank in the world. The bay contains the largest number of seagrass species ever recorded in one place. The bay has a higher salinity than the ocean waters. It contains stromatolites, modern equivalents of the earliest signs of life on earth. Aborigines have lived in the area for over 20,000 years. Today, the site is located in the Gascoyne administrative region of Western Australia.

Located in southwestern New South Wales, the **Willandra Lakes Region** is the traditional meeting place of the Muthi Muthi, Nyiampaar, and Barkinji Aboriginal tribes. A small section of the region is protected by Mungo National Park, which includes the world's oldest cremation site. Lake Mungo is one of seventeen lakes in the region. It was the site of many important archaeological findings, including Mungo Man, the oldest human remains found in Australia, and Mungo Lady, the oldest human remains in the world to be ritually cremated. It is the location of the Lake Mungo geomagnetic excursion.

An irregularly crescent-shaped volcanic remnant in the Tasman Sea between Australia and New Zealand 370 miles east of Port Macquarie and 560 miles from Norfolk Island, **Lord Howe Island** is part of a larger group of 28 islands, islets, and rocks. The volcanic and uninhabited Ball's Pyramid is the most notable of these, located fourteen miles southeast of the main island. Most of the island is virtually untouched forest with many endemic species of flora and fauna. The world's southernmost barrier coral reef can also be found here. Scuba diving, birdwatching, snorkeling, surfing, kayaking, and fishing are popular tourist activities on the island. 202 different bird species have been recorded on the island, and the large forest bat is the only native mammal on the island. The Lord Howe Island stick insect was thought to be extinct by 1920 until it was rediscovered in 2001. It now lives on Ball's Pyramid, an erosional remnant of a shield volcano and caldera. Only 24 individuals remained when it was rediscovered. Marine environments in the group are nearly pristine and highly biodiverse due to the East Australian Current. 490 fish species have been recorded, thirteen of them endemic. Whales used to be abundant in the island waters but were reduced to near-extinction in the 1960s and 1970s. The worldwide exporting of *Howea belmoreana*, the kentia palm, is important to the island's economy.

# fiji

# fiji

## Political Geography

**Capital** Suva

**Four Largest Divisions (Area)** Western, Northern, Central, Eastern

**Four Largest Divisions (Population)** Central, Western, Northern, Eastern

**Five Largest Provinces (Area)** Cakaudrove (Northern), Ba (Western), Nadroga-Navosa (Western), Macuata (Northern), Naitasiri (Central)

**Five Largest Provinces (Population)** Ba (Western), Naitasiri (Central), Suva (Central), Macuata (Northern), Nadroga-Navosa (Western)

## Five Largest Cities

| City | Province, Division | Tourist Attractions | Body of Water |
|---|---|---|---|
| **Nasinu** | Naitasiri, Central | N/A | N/A |
| **Suva** | Rewa, Central | Thurston Gardens, Colo-i-Suva Forest Reserve, Fiji Museum, Mount Tomanivi, ANZ National Stadium, Nukulau | Laucala Bay, Suva Harbour |
| **Lautoka** | Ba, Western | N/A | Pacific Ocean |

| Nadi | Ba, Western | Denarau Island, Mamanuca Islands, Kula Eco Park, Sri Siva Subramaniya temple, Nananu-i-Ra, Yasawa | Nadi River, Nadi Bay |
| --- | --- | --- | --- |
| Nausori | Tailevu, Central | N/A | Pacific Ocean |

## Physical Geography

**Relative Size** Slightly larger than Kuwait or half the size of Guinea-Bissau

**Highest Point** An extinct volcano in the northern highlands of the island of Viti Levu, **Mount Tomanivi** is the highest point in Fiji at 4,344 feet above sea level. The Rewa, Navua, Sigatoka, and Ba Rivers all have their headwaters in the area.

**Lowest Point** Pacific Ocean

## Volcanoes

### Rotuma (see Islands)

An elongated shield volcano on Taveuni, the third largest island in Fiji, **Mount Taveuni** contains the highest peak on the island, Mount Uluigalau. It could threaten the entire island if it erupted, although it leaves behind rich volcanic soils for farming that gave Taveuni the nickname of the "Garden Island of Fiji".

# Islands

The largest island in Fiji, **Viti Levu** is the site of Suva, the country's capital, and Nasinu, its largest city. It is home to seventy percent of the Fijian population, and it is the hub of the entire archipelago, slightly smaller than Connecticut. The island is comprised of eight of Fiji's fourteen provinces. Geologists believe that it has been covered by lava and other volcanic materials several times, and it includes the country's highest peak, Mount Tomanivi (formerly named Mount Victoria). It is the only known home of the giant Fijian long-horned beetle. According to tradition, Viseisei, in the northwestern sector of the island, was the first settlement established in Fiji. Sugarcane production thrives in the west, separated by a mountain range from the dairy-producing east.

The second largest island of Fiji, **Vanua Levu** lies forty miles to the north of Viti Levu. It lies to the north of the Koro Sea, and it is divided by a mountain range separating Cakaudrove and Macuata Provinces. Mount Batini is the highest point, and the Dreketi River is the deepest river in the country. Labasa is the largest settlement on the island, while Savusavu is a popular tourist destination for its diving and yachting facilities. The island is divided into Bua, Macuata, and Cakaudrove Provinces, and along with the Lau Islands, it forms the Tovata Confederacy, one of the three traditional alliances of Fiji's chiefs. In 2012, Kiribati began negotiating to buy part of the island to house its population due to rising sea levels.

The third largest island in Fiji after Vanua Levu and Viti Levu, **Taveuni** is a massive shield volcano rising from the floor of the Pacific Ocean four miles east of Vanua Levu across the Somosomo Strait. It is part of Cakaudrove Province, and it is known as the "Garden Island of Fiji" for its excellent diving opportunities, prolific bird life, bushwalks, and waterfalls. The island lies at the northern end of the Koro Sea, and its highest point is Mount Uluigalau, the second highest point in the country after Mount Tomanivi. Lake Tagimaucia is a popular tourist attraction, home to the rare tagimaucia flower. Bouma Falls are the most famous waterfalls in Fiji, and the largest settlement is Waiyevo. Naqara, an Indo-Fijian settlement, is the commercial center. The critically endangered red-throated lorikeet can be found on the island. Copra, taro, kava, vanilla, fruit, and coffee are the main crops.

The fourth largest island in Fiji, **Kadavu Island** is the largest island of the Kadavu Group, an archipelago south of Viti Levu surrounded by the Great Astrolabe Reef, one of the country's premier scuba diving locations. Vunisea is the administrative center of the island, which has two sections connected by the narrow Namalata Isthmus separating Namalata Bay in the north from Galoa Harbour in the south. Nabukelevu is the highest point of the island, which is home to the endemic velvet dove, crimson shining parrot, Kadavu honeyeater, and Kadavu fantail.

A dependency of Fiji 400 miles north of Suva, **Rotuma** is home to the small but unique Rotuman ethnic group. Ahau is the capital of the island, which is a shield volcano with its highest point at Satarua Peak. The people of the island are much different from those of Viti Levu and Vanua Levu, and tensions still remain.

## Archipelagos

An archipelago just east of the Koro Sea, the **Lau Islands** consist of high volcanic islands in the north and low carbonate islands in the south. They form the Lau Province of eastern Fiji, and unlike the rest of the country, cricket is the most popular sport. Moala Island is the largest island in the archipelago, and the largest settlement is Tubou, on Lakeba. Lakeba was a traditional meeting place between Tongans and Fijians in the past.

Consisting of seven main islands and several smaller ones, the **Lomaiviti Islands** form the Lomaiviti Province of eastern Fiji. The largest town in the archipelago is Levuka, the first capital of the country and its only UNESCO World Heritage Site. Gau Island is the largest of the islands in the archipelago.

A volcanic archipelago west of the city of Nadi and south of the Yasawa Islands, the **Mamanuca Islands** consist of about twenty islands. Port Denarau is the gateway to the archipelago, which is popular for sailing, swimming, snorkeling, kayaking, coral viewing, diving, windsurfing, and hiking. Malolo is the largest island of the archipelago.

An archipelago of about twenty volcanic islands in western Fiji, the **Yasawa Islands** consist of six main islands and several smaller islets. Yasawa is the main island of the group, and Nabukeru is the largest settlement. Tourism has been popular since the 1950s.

## Rivers

| River | Source | Mouth | Cities (if any) |
|---|---|---|---|
| **Rewa (Viti Levu)** | Mount Tomanivi | Laucala Bay | N/A |
| **Sigatoka (Viti Levu)** | Mount Tomanivi | Pacific Ocean | N/A |
| **Dreketi (Vanua Levu)** | Vanua Levu | Pacific Ocean | Sigatoka |
| **Nadi (Viti Levu)** | Viti Levu | Pacific Ocean | Nadi |
| **Ba (Viti Levu)** | Mount Tomanivi | Pacific Ocean | Ba |

## Seas

A sea of the Pacific Ocean between Viti Levu, the largest island in Fiji, to the west and the Lau Islands to the east, the **Koro Sea** is named after Koro Island, the third largest of the Lau Islands and the seventh largest island in the country.

## Straits

The strait separating Taveuni Island and Vanua Levu, the **Somosomo Strait** is known for its soft coral. It is a popular diving location.

## Economic Geography

**Currency** Fijian dollar

**Natural Resources** Timber, fish, gold, copper, petroleum, hydropower

**Agricultural Products** Sugarcane, coconuts, cassava, rice, sweet potatoes, bananas, ginger, taro, kava

**Ports** Suva (largest port), Nadi

## Historical Geography

**Former Capital** Levuka (1874-1877)

**Historic Cities** Levuka (est. 1820), Suva (est. 1868)

**Empires** Kingdom of Fiji (1871-1874), British Empire (1874-1970)

**Natives** Fijians

**Independence** From the United Kingdom, 1970

## Cultural Geography

**Language** English, Fijian, Hindi (official)

**Major Ethnic Groups** Fijian (49.9%), Fijian Indian (46.2%), Euronesian (1.7%), Rotuman (1.2%), Pacific Islander (1%), European (0.7%), Chinese (0.7%)

**Religion** Methodist (34.8%), Catholic (9.1%), Assemblies of God (5.7%), Seventh-Day Adventist (3.9%), Anglican (0.8%), other Christian (10.1%), Sanatānī (23%), other Hindu (6.9%), Muslim (5.3%), Sikh (0.4%)

**Foods** Kokoda, palusami, baigan valo

# Destinations

## National Parks

**Sigatoka Sand Dunes National Park** (see Tourist Attractions)

## Tourist Attractions

An ecological preserve near the town of Sigatoka on Viti Levu, **Kula Eco Park** was originally established as a bird park in the 1980s. It preserves Fiji's indigenous flora and fauna, including the Fijian monkey-faced bat, the only native mammal in the country. The park is also home to the Fiji crested iguana, Fiji banded iguana, Kadavu musk parrot, Pacific black duck, and Fiji ground frog.

A small private island three miles northwest of Nadi, the fourth largest city in Fiji, **Denarau Island** is the main starting point for trips to the Mamanuca and Yasawa Islands. It is known for its hotels and resorts, and it is accessible, just a few miles from Nadi International Airport, the country's main airport.

Located at the mouth of the Sigatoka River on the island of Viti Levu two miles west of the town of Sigatoka, the **Sigatoka Sand Dunes** were created by erosion. They were designated as Fiji's first national park in 1989, and they are a key tourist destination.

A nature reserve near Suva, the capital and second largest city of Fiji, the **Colo-I-Suva Forest Reserve** was established in 1872. The Waisila Creek flows through the park into the Waimanu River. The reserve protects an area of rainforests renowned for their tropical flora and birds.

A Hindu temple in Nadi, the fourth largest city in Fiji, the **Sri Siva Subramaniya Temple** is the largest Hindu temple in the Southern Hemisphere. It was built in the 1980s in the Dravidian style, having been founded in 1976.

**Mamanuca Islands** (see Archipelagos)

A small island off the southwestern coast of Viti Levu, **Robinson Crusoe Island** was first known as Likuri Island. Pottery found on the island dates back to 1500 BE, and it is a traditional location among the Lapita people for ceremonies and chiefly gatherings. It has recently become home to a small resort, a short distance south of Nadi. The island was named after the story of Robinson Crusoe after a sailing yacht was wrecked on the nearby reef and the captain and his cat took refuge on the island. It lies in the estuary of the Tuva River.

An island two miles off the northern coat of Viti Levu near the town of Rakiraki in Ra Province, **Nananu-I-Ra** is said to be where disembodied spirits leave the world for the afterlife in Fijian mythology. It is a popular kitesurfing and windsurfing destination due to consistent trade winds from April to October. Oni Beach is the most beautiful beach on the island.

**Yasawa Islands** (see Archipelagos)

A small islet six miles east of Suva, the capital and largest city of Fiji, **Nukulau** was bought by John Brown Williams, an American, in 1846. His house was burnt down in 1849, leading to the First Fiji Expedition by the American army in 1855 and later the Second Fiji Expedition in 1858. The island was ceded to the United Kingdom in 1874. From 1879 to 1916, it served as a quarantine center for thousands of Indian indentured laborers who were later employed on the country's sugar plantations.

## World Heritage Sites

A town on the eastern coast of the island of Ovalau, the second largest island of the Lomaiviti Archipelago, **Levuka** is the largest settlement and the economic hub of the island. It was founded around 1820 by European settlers and traders as the first modern town in Fiji, and it became an important port and trading post. When the first modern Fijian state was founded in 1871, Seru Epenisa Cakobau was crowned king in the town. Following the British annexation of the archipelago, the town remained the capital until 1877, when the administration was moved to Suva. The Fiji Times, the country's oldest newspaper, was founded in the town in 1869. Today, the town is the site of the Levuka Community Centre, which houses a branch of the Fiji Museum, and the Sacred Heart Church, built in 1858.

# kiribati

# kiribati

## Political Geography

**Capital** South Tarawa

## Five Largest Cities

| City | Tourist Attractions | Body of Water |
|------|---------------------|---------------|
| South Tarawa | N/A | Pacific Ocean |
| Betio | N/A | Pacific Ocean |
| Bikenibeu | N/A | Pacific Ocean |
| North Tarawa | N/A | Pacific Ocean |
| Butaritari | N/A | Pacific Ocean |

## Physical Geography

**Relative Size** Slightly smaller than Tonga or half the size of the Faroe Islands

**Highest Point** Unnamed location on Banaba Island (266 feet above sea level)

**Lowest Point** Pacific Ocean

## Islands and Atolls

A raised coral atoll in the northern Line Islands, **Kiritimati** is the largest coral atoll in the world, comprising seventy percent of Kiribati's land area. It lies 1,340 miles south of Honolulu in the world's farthest forward time zone, UTC+14, making it one of the first inhabited places on the planet to experience the New Year, the other being Caroline Island, also in Kiribati. The lagoon within the atoll opens up into the Pacific Ocean in the northwest through the Burgle Channel. Vaskess Bay extends along the southwestern coast of the atoll. Joe's Hill is the highest point. The atoll was uninhabited at the time of its discovery by the Spanish explorer Hernando de Grijalva in 1537. The United States claimed the atoll under the Guano Islands Act of 1856. Permanent settlement began in 1882, but due to an extreme drought which killed off tens of thousands of coconut palms, it was abandoned once again from 1905 to 1912. In World War II, it was held by the allies. During the Cold War, there was nuclear bomb testing in the area. The Treaty of Tarawa, signed in 1979 and ratified in 1983, gave the atoll to Kiribati. Tabwakea is the largest settlement on the atoll, which is accessible via Cassidy International Airport. The bokikokiko is a species of warbler only found on the atoll. Only Polynesian rats and goats are native to the atoll. Many other rare species can be found on the atoll.

A low, arid, and uninhabited island in the central Pacific Ocean, **Malden Island** is one of the Line Islands. It lies 1,761 miles south of Honolulu, and the nearest inhabited place is Penrhyn, one of the Cook Islands. There is no fresh water on the island, which is an important breeding site for about a dozen bird species. The island was discovered by George Byron in 1825, and although it was uninhabited, the remains of ruined temples and other structures were found. Under the Guano Islands Act of 1856, the island was claimed by the United States. However, before the U. S. Guano Company could begin exploiting the island, it was occupied by an Australian company under a British license. In 1956, the United Kingdom selected the island for its first series of H-bomb tests. In 1975, it was reserved as a wildlife sanctuary, administered from Kiritimati.

The capital of Kiribati, **Tarawa** consists of North Tarawa, which has more in common with the other islands of the Gilbert Islands, and South Tarawa, home to half of the country's population. The atoll has a large lagoon, and breadfruit, papayas, bananas, coconuts, and pandanus are grown. It is best known for having been the site of the bloody Battle of Tarawa, the first American offensive in the central Pacific region in World War II.

A solitary raised coral island 185 miles east of Nauru and west of the Gilbert Islands, **Banaba Island** contains the highest point in Kiribati. Along with Nauru and Makatea, in French Polynesia, the island is one of the three important elevated phosphate-rich islands of the Pacific. Phosphate mining from 1900 to 1979 stripped away ninety percent of the island's surface, and only 335 people remain after most of the population was relocated to Rabi Island in northern Fiji. Many Banabans have called for the island to secede from Kiribati and become part of Fiji, stating that Kiribati is planning to mine the island for its own enrichment. The island is also important to Kiribati because, unlike the rest of the country, it is less susceptible to rising sea levels.

## Archipelagos

A chain of sixteen atolls and coral islands in the Pacific Ocean, the **Gilbert Islands** are arranged in a north-to-south line 484 miles long, stretching from Makin in the north to Arorae in the south. Tabiteuea is the largest atoll in the chain, while Tarawa is the most populous. The islands were named after Thomas Gilbert, who passed through them in 1788. A British protectorate was proclaimed over the islands in 1892, and in 1915, the Gilbert and Ellice Islands were made a colony of the British Empire. The natives of the islands are Micronesian. Coconuts, pandanus, and taro are grown in the archipelago.

A group of eight atolls and two submerged coral reefs east of the Gilbert Islands and west of the Line Islands, the **Phoenix Islands** are protected by the Phoenix Islands Protected Area, one of the largest protected areas in the world and a UNESCO World Heritage Site. Kanton Island is the largest, northernmost, and only inhabited island of the archipelago, while Nikumaroro is said to be where Amelia Earhart's plane crashed in 1937. The islands were discovered in the early 19th century by whalers. They were annexed by the United Kingdom in the late 19th century, although the United States claimed Howland and Baker Islands, northern outliers of the archipelago, in 1935. Today, the islands are known for their 120 species of coral and over 500 species of fish, which were protected in 2006.

A chain of eleven atolls and low coral islands in the central Pacific Ocean stretching 1,460 miles in a northwest-to-southeast line, the **Line Islands** are one of the longest island chains in the world. Eight of the islands are part of Kiribati, while the other three are members of the United States Minor Outlying Islands. The I-Kiribati part of the archipelago has the farthest forward time zone in the world. Kiritimati is by far the largest atoll in the archipelago (and the largest atoll in the world), followed by Malden Island. Jarvis Island is the largest American island.

## Economic Geography

**Currency** Kiribati dollar, Australian dollar

**Natural Resources** Fish

**Agricultural Products** Copra, taro, breadfruit, sweet potatoes, vegetables

**Port** Tarawa

## Historical Geography

**Empires** British Empire (1892-1979)

**Natives** Micronesians

**Independence** From the United Kingdom, 1979

## Cultural Geography

**Language** English, Gilbertese (official)

**Major Ethnic Groups** Micronesian (98.8%), other (1.2%)

**Religion** Roman Catholic (55.8%), Kiribati Uniting Church (33.5%), Mormon (4.7%), Bahá'í (2.3%), Adventist (2%), other (1.7%)

**Foods** Fish, copra, taro, breadfruit, sweet potatoes, vegetables

# Destinations

## World Heritage Sites

Protecting the Phoenix Islands, one of Kiribati's three archipelagos, the **Phoenix Islands Protected Area** consists of eleven percent of the country's Exclusive Economic Zone. It is one of the largest marine protected areas in the world at the size of California. The area protects 514 species of reed fish, and several species of birds nest on the islands within the archipelago.

# marshall islands

# marshall islands

## Political Geography

**Capital** Majuro

**Five Largest Municipalities (Area):** Kwajalein, Mili, Ailinglaplap, Arno, Jaluit

**Five Largest Municipalities (Population):** Majuro, Kwajalein, Arno, Ailinglaplap, Jaluit

## Five Largest Cities

| City | Municipality | Tourist Attractions | Body of Water |
|------|-------------|---------------------|---------------|
| **Majuro** | Majuro | N/A | Pacific Ocean |
| **Ebeye** | Kwajalein | N/A | Pacific Ocean |
| **Rairok** | Majuro | N/A | Pacific Ocean |
| **Ajeltake** | Majuro | N/A | Pacific Ocean |
| **Laura** | Majuro | N/A | Pacific Ocean |

## Physical Geography

**Relative Size** About the size of Aruba or American Samoa

**Highest Point** Unnamed location on Likiep Atoll (33 feet above sea level)

**Lowest Point** Pacific Ocean

## Atolls

The largest atoll in the Marshall Islands by area, **Kwajalein** consists of 97 islands and islets. The two main islands are Kwajalein Island, the southernmost and largest island, and Ebeye Island, the most populous island. The atoll surrounds one of the largest lagoons in the world. It was the site of heavy fighting during World War II and is located in the Ralik Chain.

## Archipelagos

The western chain of the Marshall Islands, the **Ralik Chain** contains the country's largest atoll of Kwajalein. The name of the archipelago means "sunset" in Marshallese.

The eastern chain of the Marshall Islands, the **Ratak Chain** contains the country's most populous atoll of Majuro. The name of the archipelago means "sunrise" in Marshallese.

## Straits

Separating Knox Atoll from Mili Atoll, the **Klee Passage** is a shallow channel of water located directly above a sand bank. The atolls used to be connected through this sand bank.

## Economic Geography

**Currency** United States dollar

**Natural Resources** Coconut products, marine products, deep seabed minerals

**Agricultural Products** Fish, breadfruit, banana, taro, pandanus

**Port** Majuro

# Historical Geography

**Former Capital** Jabur (1885-1944)

**Empires** Spanish Empire (1874-1885), German Empire (1885-1914), Empire of Japan (1914-1944)

**Natives** Micronesians

**Independence** From the United States: 1979 (self-government) and 1986 (Compact of Free Association)

# Cultural Geography

**Language** Marshallese, English (official)

**Major Ethnic Groups** Marshallese (92.1%), mixed Marshallese (5.9%), other (2%)

**Religion** United Church of Christ (51.5%), Assemblies of God (24.2%), Roman Catholic (8.4%), Mormon (8.3%), Bukot Nan Jesus (2.2%), Baptist (1%), Seventh-day Adventist (0.9%), Full Gospel (0.7%), Bahá'í (0.6%), other or irreligious (2.2%)

**Foods** Fish, coconuts, breadfruit, bananas, taro, pandanus

# Destinations

## World Heritage Sites

Formerly known as Escholtz Atoll, **Bikini Atoll** was the site of the detonation of 23 nuclear devices by the United States. The atoll contains 23 islands and is not populated due to the radioactivity that can still be found there.

# micronesia

# micronesia

## Political Geography

**Capital** Palikir

**Four Largest States (Area)** Pohnpei, Chuuk, Yap, Kosrae

**Four Largest States (Population)** Chuuk, Pohnpei, Yap, Kosrae

## Five Largest Cities

| City | State | Tourist Attractions | Body of Water |
|------|-------|---------------------|---------------|
| **Weno** | Chuuk | N/A | Pou Bay, Chuuk Lagoon, Pacific Ocean |
| **Tofol** | Kosrae | N/A | Pacific Ocean |
| **Colonia** | Yap | N/A | Pacific Ocean |
| **Kolonia** | Pohnpei | N/A | Pacific Ocean |
| **Palikir** | Pohnpei | N/A | Pacific Ocean |

## Physical Geography

**Relative Size** Slightly larger than Bahrain or half the size of the Faroe Islands

**Highest Point** Located on the island of Pohnpei, **Mount Nanlaud** is the highest point of Micronesia at 2,566 feet above sea level. It is also the second highest mountain in the region of Micronesia after Agrihan in the Northern Mariana Islands.

**Lowest Point** Pacific Ocean

# Islands and Atolls

An atoll in Chuuk State about 1,100 miles northeast of New Guinea, **Chuuk** consists of a protective reef enclosing a natural harbor. Weno, on the island of Weno, is the capital and largest city of the atoll and the largest city in Micronesia. Widespread human settlements appeared in the atoll's islands in the 14th century, and the first recorded European sighting was by the Spanish explorer Álvaro de Saavedra Cerón in 1528. The Spanish claimed the atoll until 1899, when the Caroline Islands were sold to the German Empire. In World War II, the atoll was the Empire of Japan's main base in the South Pacific. In Operation Hailstone in 1944, American planes sank 44 Japanese ships and destroyed 275 aircraft in the atoll. Today, the islands of the atoll grow copra, and scuba diving among its wrecks is a popular tourist activity.

Forming one of the states of Micronesia, **Kosrae** is the easternmost of the Caroline Islands. It lies 370 miles north of the Equator, and Tofol is its capital and largest settlement. The island is largely unspoiled, and it is becoming a scuba diving and hiking destination. It was first sighted by Álvaro de Saavedra Cerón in 1529, although it was not effectively occupied until 1885. Breadfruit, coconuts, bananas, taro, yam, and sugarcane are grown on the island.

An island of the Senyavin Islands of the Caroline Islands in Pohnpei State, **Pohnpei** has its capital at Kolonia and Palikir, the capital of Micronesia. It is the largest, highest, most populous, and most developed island in the country, home to the endemic Pohnpei lorikeet, Pohnpei fantail, Pohnpei flycatcher, and long-billed white-eye. The island passed through Spanish, German, and Japanese hands before becoming an American trust territory. The population is a melting pot of indigenous people, Europeans, and Asians.

A group of four islands in the Caroline Islands, Yap consists of Yap Island proper, Gagil-Tamil, Maap, and Rumung. Colonia is the capital of the islands and the largest settlement, located on the main island. The islands were part of the Captaincy General of the Philippines from the 17th century to 1899, when they were sold to Germany. They are known for their Rai stones, a form of currency made of large, carved doughnut-shaped disks of calcite. The islands' indigenous cultures and traditions are strong compared to other Micronesian states.

## Archipelagos

A widely scattered archipelago of tiny islands in the northwestern Pacific ocean north of New Guinea, the **Caroline Islands** are divided between Micronesia in the east and Palau in the west. Most of the islands are part of low, flat coral atolls. They were first sighted by Europeans in the early 16th century and claimed by the Spanish. After the Spanish-American War of 1898, the islands were sold to Germany in the German-Spanish treaty. They were invaded and occupied by Japan in both world wars, and after World War II, they became trust territories of the United States, with Micronesia gaining independence in 1986 and Palau in 1994.

## Seas

Northeast of the Philippine Archipelago, northwest of Palau, Yap, and Ulithi of Micronesia, west of the Mariana Islands, southwest of Bonin and Iwo Jima, south of Honshu, Shikoku, and Kyushu, southeast of the Ryukyu Islands, and east of Taiwan, the **Philippine Sea** contains the Philippine Trench, the third lowest point on Earth. Island arcs extend above the ocean surface due to plate tectonics in the area.

## Economic Geography

**Currency** United States dollar

**Natural Resources** Wood, lumber, minerals, phosphate

**Agricultural Products** Black pepper, tropical fruits, vegetables, coconuts, cassava, sweet potatoes

**Ports** Weno, Palikir (largest port)

# Historical Geography

**Former Capital** Kolonia (1914-1989)

**Historic City** Kolonia (est. 1887)

**Empires** Saudeleur Dynasty (1100-1628), Spanish Empire (16th century-1899), German Empire (1899-1919), Empire of Japan (1919-1922, 1941-1944)

**Natives** Chuukese, Pohnpeian, Kosraean, Yapese, Outer Yapese

**Independence** From the United States, 1979

# Cultural Geography

**Language** English (official and national), Chuukese, Kosraean, Pohnpeian, Yapese (recognized regionally)

**Major Ethnic Groups** Chuukese (48.2%), Pohnpeian (24.2%), Kosraean (6.2%), Yapese (5.2%), Outer Yapese (4.5%), Asian (1.8%), Polynesian (1.5%), other (7.8%)

**Religion** Protestant, Roman Catholic, other Christian, Buddhist

**Foods** Fish, coconuts, cassava, bananas, sweet potatoes

# Destinations

# Tourist Attractions

**Chuuk Lagoon** (see Major Islands and Atolls)

**Nan Madol** (see World Heritage Sites)

A small atoll off the western coast of Pohnpei in the Senyavin Islands, **Ant Atoll** was first visited by the Spanish explorer Álvaro de Saavedra Cerón in 1529. Today, it is a popular site with tourists for diving and snorkeling, and it is a seabird colony.

The capital of Pohnpei State, **Kolonia** was the capital of all of Micronesia from 1914 to 1989. It is the largest population center on the island of Pohnpei and its commercial hub. Germans built roads, wharfs, and buildings in the settlement after taking control of the island in 1899. The Japanese brought thousands of Okinawans to the island in World War I. During World War II, much of the town was destroyed by American bombs. Today, the town is home to state government offices, schools, stores, restaurants, hotels, and places of worship.

A major prehistoric and historic archaeological site on Lelu Island in Kosrae State, **Leluh** is the remains of a civilization that peaked around the 14th and 15th centuries. Its rulers gradually conquered and unified the island of Kosrae, and they ruled with a monarchy similar to the kingdoms of Tonga and Hawaii. The site is built of coral and basalt, similar to Nan Madol.

A small atoll off the northwestern coast of Pohnpei in the Senyavin Islands, **Pakin Atoll** has a small population. It is a popular site with tourists for diving and snorkeling.

## World Heritage Sites

A ruined city on the eastern shore of the island of Pohnpei, **Nan Madol** was the capital of the Saudeleur Dynasty, the first organized government uniting the people of the island, until 1628. It consists of a series of small artificial islands linked by a network of canals, giving it the nickname "Venice of the Pacific". It lies between the main island of Pohnpei and Temwen Island, and it was a center of human activity as early as the 1st or 2nd century. Its distinctive megalithic architecture, however, was not built until the 12th or 13th century. The reign of the Saudeleur rulers ended with the invasion of the island by Isokelekel, who came from Kosrae.

# nauru

# nauru

## Political Geography

**Capital** Yaren (*de facto*)

**Five Largest Districts (Area)** Anibare, Meneng, Buada, Nibok, Anabar

**Five Largest Districts (Population)** Denigomodu, Meneng, Aiwo, Boe, Yaren

## Five Largest Cities

| City | District | Tourist Attractions | Body of Water |
|------|----------|---------------------|---------------|
| **Denigomodu** | Denigomodu | N/A | Pacific Ocean |
| **Meneng** | Meneng | N/A | Pacific Ocean |
| **Aiwo** | Aiwo | N/A | Pacific Ocean |
| **Boe** | Boe | N/A | Pacific Ocean |
| **Yaren** | Yaren | N/A | Moqua Well, Pacific Ocean |

## Physical Geography

**Highest Point** Located in the Aiwo District of western Nauru, the **Command Ridge** is the highest point in the country at 213 feet above sea level.

**Lowest Point** Pacific Ocean

## Islands

**Nauru** (the entire country is an island)

## Lakes

A slightly brackish freshwater lake in the Buada District of central Nauru, the **Buada Lagoon** is an endorheic lake surrounded by trees, unlike the rest of the country.

## Bays

A large bay in the Anibare District of eastern Nauru, **Anibare Bay** is bordered by capes to the north and south in the Ijuw and Meneng Districts, respectively. It is popular with tourists.

## Economic Geography

**Currency** Australian dollar

**Natural Resources** Phosphates

**Agricultural Products** Coconuts

**Port** The whole country

## Historical Geography

**Former Name** Pleasant Island

**Empires** German Empire (1888-1942), Empire of Japan (1942-1943)

**Natives** Nauruans

**Independence** From the United Kingdom, Australia, and New Zealand, 1968

# Cultural Geography

**Language** English (official and national), Chuukese, Kosraean, Pohnpeian, Yapese (recognized regionally)

**Major Ethnic Groups** Nauruan (58%), other Pacific Islander (26%), European (8%), Chinese (8%)

**Religion** Nauru Congregational Church (35.7%), Roman Catholic (33%), Assemblies of God (13%), indigenous religion (9.5%), Baptist (1.5%), other (7.3%)

**Foods** Coconuts, fish

# Destinations

## Tourist Attractions

**Anibare Bay** (see Bays)

**Buada Lagoon** (see Lakes)

**Command Ridge** (see Highest Point)

# new zealand

# new zealand

## Political Geography

**Sobriquet** Land of the Long White Cloud

**Capital** Wellington

**Five Largest Regions (Area)** Canterbury, Southland, Otago, Waikato, West Coast

**Five Largest Regions (Population)** Auckland, Canterbury, Wellington, Waikato, Bay of Plenty

## Five Largest Cities

| City | Region | Tourist Attractions | Body of Water |
|------|--------|---------------------|---------------|
| **Auckland** | Auckland | Sky Tower, Kelly Tarlton's Sea Life Aquarium, Museum of Transport and Technology, Auckland Art Gallery, Eden Park | Tamaki River, Manukau Harbor, Waitemata Harbor, Hauraki Gulf |
| **Wellington** | Wellington | Museum of New Zealand Te Papa Tongarewa, Zealandia, Museum of Wellington City and Sea, Wellington Botanic Garden | Lambton Harbor, Wellington Harbor, Cook Strait |

| City | Region | Tourist Attractions | Body of Water |
|---|---|---|---|
| **Christchurch** | Canterbury | Christchurch Botanic Gardens, International Antarctic Centre, Willowbank Wildlife Reserve, Canterbury Museum | Avon River, Heathcote River, Waimakariri River, Pegasus Bay, Pacific Ocean |
| **Hamilton** | Waikato | N/A | Waikato River, Lake Rotoroa |
| **Tauranga** | Bay of Plenty | N/A | Tauranga Harbor, Bay of Plenty |

# Physical Geography

**Relative Size** Slightly larger than Gabon or Colorado

**Highest Point** Located in the Southern Alps of South Island, **Mount Cook (Aoraki)** is the highest point of New Zealand at 12,218 feet above sea level. It is situated between the Hooker Glacier to the west and the Tasman Glacier to the east. It is part of Aoraki/Mount Cook National Park, part of the Te Wahipounamu World Heritage Site. The peak is also a favorite challenge for mountain climbers.

**Lowest Point** An area of fertile agricultural land southwest of Dunedin, the **Taieri Plains** are the lowest point of New Zealand at seven feet below sea level. The Taieri and Waipori Rivers flow through the area. Dairy and sheep farming dominate the agriculture of the plains.

## Deserts

Located in the central part of North Island, the **Rangipo Desert** receives about 80 inches of rainfall per year but still resembles a desert due to poor soil quality and dry winds. Mount Ruapehu, the highest point of North Island, is situated near the desert. The Waikato and Whangaehu Rivers have their sources in the area. Scenes from the Lord of the Rings films were shot in the desert.

## Plateaus

Often called the Central Plateau and occasionally the Waimarino Plateau, the **North Island Volcanic Plateau** covers much of central North Island with volcanoes and crater lakes. It is home to Lake Taupo, the largest lake in New Zealand, and Ruapehu, the tallest mountain of North Island. The Waikato and Whanganui Rivers have their sources on the plateau.

## Volcanoes

A volcanic seamount south of Tonga, the **Monowai Seamount** is one of the most active volcanoes in the Kermadec volcanic arc. In 2012, a floating raft of pumice was found offshore New Zealand but was not actually from the seamount.

## Mountain Ranges

Located in the southwestern part of South Island, the **Hunter Mountains** extend from Lake Manapouri to Green Lake in Fiordland National Park. The Manapouri Hydroelectric Power Station is located near the range.

Consisting of two parallel ranges in the northeastern part of South Island, the **Kaikoura Ranges** are separated by the valley of the Clarence River. The Awatere River on the other side of the western Kaikoura Ranges runs parallel to the Clarence River.

Located in the eastern part of North Island, the **Kaweka Range** runs between the city of Napier and Lake Taupo. Many of the rivers that have their sources in the range flow into Hawke Bay. The Kaweka Challenge is a group of races held in the mountain range.

The largest of the mountain ranges of North Island, the **Ruahine Range** runs parallel to the east coast of the island. Mangaweka is the second highest non-volcanic peak of the island while Whariti has a highly visible television transmission tower.

Extending along much of the length of the western part of South Island, the **Southern Alps** contain Mount Cook (Aoraki), the highest point in New Zealand. The Tasman Glacier is the longest glacier in the mountain range. Most of the range is protected through national parks such as Westland Tai Poutini, Mount Aspiring, and Aoraki/Mount Cook National Parks. 25% of New Zealand's plant species are found in alpine habitats such as that of the mountain range.

Running parallel to the east coast of North Island, the **Tararua Range** is located in the southern part of the island. The highest peak is Mitre, named so because it resembles a bishop's headgear, known as a mitre.

## Mountain Passes

**Arthur's Pass** (see National Parks)

Located between the Kakanui Mountains and the Maniototo plain, **Danseys Pass** is situated in the Otago Region. The pass is a link between the towns of Naseby and Ranfurly in the south and Duntroon in the north.

Located in the Southern Alps of the South Island, **Haast Pass** is one of the three road passes through the Southern Alps, the others being Arthur's Pass and Lewis Pass. It is situated between the valleys of the Haast and Makarora Rivers in Mount Aspiring National Park.

The northernmost of the three main road passes across the Southern Alps, **Lewis Pass** is located between the valleys of the Maruia River to the northwest and the Lewis River to the southeast. It passes through a large beech forest.

Located near Lake Lyndon in the Canterbury Region in the Southern Alps, **Porters Pass** is the third highest point on the South Island's highway network. The pass offers views of the Canterbury Plains.

Connecting Doubtful Sound, a deep indentation in the Fiordland coast, to the valley of the west arm of Lake Manapouri, the **Wilmot Pass** lies between Mount Wilmot and Mount Mainwaring. It is the only road on the New Zealand mainland (North and South Islands) disconnected from the rest of the road network.

## Valleys

A large area of flat land on the banks of the Hutt River, the **Hutt Valley** contains the cities of Upper Hutt and Lower Hutt, both part of the Wellington metropolitan area. The Hutt River flows along the course of an active geologic fault that continues south into the Southern Alps of South Island.

## Rivers

| River | Source | Mouth | Cities (if any) |
|---|---|---|---|
| **Waikato (North Island)** | Lake Taupo | Tasman Sea | Hamilton |
| **Clutha (South Island)** | Lake Wanaka | Pacific Ocean | N/A |
| **Whanganui (North Island)** | Mount Tongariro | Tasman Sea | N/A |
| **Taieri (South Island)** | Lammerlaw Ranges | Pacific Ocean | N/A |
| **Mataura (South** | Southern Alps | Pacific Ocean | N/A |

| River | Source | Mouth | Cities (if any) |
|---|---|---|---|
| Island) | | | |

## Lakes

The largest lake by surface area in New Zealand and the second largest freshwater lake in surface area in Oceania (after Lake Murray in Papua New Guinea), **Lake Taupo** is the source of the Waikato River, the country's longest river. It is noted for its large number of trout and lies in a caldera created by a supervolcanic eruption which occurred about 26,500 years ago.

The largest lake in South Island and the largest lake in Oceania by freshwater volume, **Lake Te Anau** is situated in the southwestern part of the island. Most of the lake is within Fiordland National Park of the Te Wahipounamu World Heritage Site. The Waiau River connects it to Lake Manapouri.

Located in the southwestern part of South Island, **Lake Wakatipu** is New Zealand's longest lake. It was formerly drained by the Mataura River. The lake is home to the New Zealand longfin eel, the only endemic eel in New Zealand. A mountain range known as The Remarkables is southeast of the lake.

The source of the Clutha River, **Lake Wanaka** is located in South Island. The lake is nearly a thousand feet deep. The towns of Wanaka and Albert Town are situated on the lake, which is in the Otago Region.

## Bays

Stretching from the Coromandel Peninsula in the west to Cape Runaway in the east, the **Bay of Plenty** was the site of New Zealand's worst ever environmental disaster, the 2011 Tauranga oil spill. Tauranga, the fifth largest city in the country, is located on the bay. The Bay of Plenty Region is located along the bay and incorporates some of the islands in the bay.

Stretching from the Mahia Peninsula in the northeast to Cape Kidnappers in the southwest, **Hawke Bay** indents the eastern part of North Island. The Napier-Hastings urban area is located on the bay. The town of Wairoa lies at the mouth of the Wairoa River. The Hawke's Bay Region is situated along the bay.

Located on the east coast of South Island, **Pegasus Bay** runs from the Banks Peninsula to the mouth of the Waipara River. Christchurch, New Zealand's third largest city, is situated at the southern end of the bay.

## Gulfs

Located between the Northland and Coromandel Peninsulas, the **Hauraki Gulf** is part of the Pacific Ocean. The gulf is connected to the ocean through the Colville, Cradock, and Jellicoe Channels. A string of islands guards the mouth of the Waitemata Harbor of Auckland. Rangitoto Island, a dormant volcano, is one of these islands. Great Barrier Island forms a northeastern barrier of the gulf.

## Seas

Named after the Dutch explorer Abel Janszoon Tasman, the first European to encounter Tasmania and New Zealand, the **Tasman Sea** is situated between southeastern Australia and New Zealand. It is informally referred to by Australians and New Zealanders as "The Ditch". Lord Howe and Norfolk Islands, both part of Australia, are the major islands in the sea. Auckland, Newcastle, Sydney, Wellington, and Wollongong are the major cities on the sea.

# Straits

Separating the North and South Islands, the two main islands of New Zealand, the **Cook Strait** connects the Tasman Sea in the northwest to the Pacific Ocean in the southeast. The strait is considered to have one of the most dangerous and unpredictable waters in the world. The national capital, Wellington, is located on the strait.

Separating South Island from Stewart Island (Rakiura), the **Foveaux Strait** has three bays to the north: Oreti Beach, Te Waewae Bay, and Toetoes Bay. The strait is a rough and often treacherous stretch of water.

# Isthmuses

The site of Auckland, New Zealand's largest city, the **Auckland Isthmus** separates the Tasman Sea from the Hauraki Gulf and connects the main portion of North Island to the Northland Peninsula. Waitemata Harbor, an arm of the Hauraki Gulf, is to the east, while Manukau Harbor, an arm of the Tasman Sea, is to the west. It is part of the Auckland volcanic field and makes up Auckland City, a former local authority district.

# Peninsulas

A peninsula of volcanic origin on the eastern coast of South Island, the **Banks Peninsula** lies just south of the city of Christchurch. It became a European whaling center in the 1830s, nearly wiping out the native Māori population. The Banks Peninsula Track is a popular tourist attraction.

Extending for 85 kilometers from the western end of the Bay of Plenty, the **Coromandel Peninsula** forms a barrier between the Hauraki Gulf and the Firth of Thames in the west to the Pacific Ocean to the east. On a clear day, the peninsula is visible from Auckland, New Zealand's largest city. It is steep, hilly, and mostly covered in temperate rainforest.

Located in far northern North Island, the **Northland Peninsula** is joined to the rest of the island by the Auckland isthmus. Its northern section is the Aupouri Peninsula, containing the Surville Cliffs, the northernmost point of mainland New Zealand. Waitangi, the site of the Treaty of Waitangi, is located on the peninsula. Whangarei is the largest settlement outside the Auckland conurbation.

A long and hilly peninsula forming the easternmost part of Dunedin on South Island, the **Otago Peninsula** is volcanic in origin. It is home to various species of endemic, rare, and endangered wildlife, and it is a popular ecotourism destination.

## Capes

The northwestern tip of the Aupouri Peninsula, the northern portion of the Northland Peninsula on North Island, **Cape Reinga** is a popular tourist attraction separating the Tasman Sea to the west from the Pacific Ocean to the east. It is an important place in Māori mythology.

## Economic Geography

**Currency** New Zealand dollar (kiwi)

**Natural Resources** Natural gas, iron ore, sand, coal, timber, hydropower, gold, limestone

**Agricultural Products** Wheat, barley, potatoes, pulses, fruits, vegetables, wool, beef, dairy products, fish

**Major Producer** Kiwis (third), sheep (third), wool (third)

**Ports** Auckland, Lyttelton, Napier, Nelson, New Plymouth, Port Chalmers, Tauranga (largest port), Timaru, Wellington

## Historical Geography

**Former Name** Staten Landt

**Former Capital** Russell (now Okiato, 1840-1841), Auckland (1841-1865)

**Historic Cities** Kerikeri (est. 1822), Bluff (est. 1823), Wellington (est. 1839), Auckland (est. 1840)

**Empires** British Empire (1840-1947)

**Natives** Māoris

**Independence** From the United Kingdom: 1907 (dominion status), 1947 (full sovereign status)

## Cultural Geography

**Language** English (official), Māori, New Zealand Sign Language (*de jure* official)

**Major Ethnic Groups** European (67.6%), Māori (14.6%), Asian (9.2%), Pacific (6.9%), other (1.7%)

**Religion** Roman Catholic (11.1%), Anglican (10.3%), Presbyterian (7.4%), other Christian (19.1%), irreligious (38.6%), other (13.5%)

**Foods** Rēwena parāoa, pavlova, fish and chips, meat pies, custard squares

## Destinations

## National Parks

**Abel Tasman National Park** (see Tourist Attractions)

**Aoraki/Mount Cook National Park** (see World Heritage Sites)

The first national park in the South Island and the third in New Zealand, **Arthur's Pass National Park** contains the source of the Waimakariri River. The park is popular for hiking (known as tramping in New Zealand), skiing, and mountaineering. It is one of the most dangerous national parks in the country and has Mount Murchison as its highest point.

Dominated by the dormant volcano of Mount Taranaki (Mount Egmont), **Egmont National Park** receives massive annual precipitation. A lush rainforest covers the foothills of the mountain. The Ahukawakawa Swamp is a rare high-altitude wetland containing many endemic species.

**Fiordland National Park** (see World Heritage Sites)

Centered on two large lakes, Lakes Rotoiti and Rotoroa, **Nelson Lakes National Park** is popular for camping, hiking, and fishing. The park is located in the northern part of South Island and contains many mountains and valleys.

The largest of the four national parks in the North Island, **Te Urewera National Park** is the traditional home of the Tuhoe People. It was one of the last regions to be claimed by the British during the colonization of New Zealand.

**Tongariro National Park** (see World Heritage Sites)

**Westland Tai Poutini National Park** (see World Heritage Sites)

Located in the southwestern part of North Island, **Whanganui National Park** borders the Whanganui River, which is not part of the park. It protects the habitat of several thousand North Island brown kiwis and the endangered blue duck.

# Tourist Attractions

**Coromandel Peninsula** (see Peninsulas)

Located between Golden Bay and Tasman Bay at the northern end of South Island, **Abel Tasman National Park** was where Abel Tasman, the first European to sight New Zealand, anchored his ship. Petrels, shags, penguins, gulls, terns, and herons frequent the park.

An observation and telecommunications tower in the Auckland Central Business District, **Sky Tower** is the tallest man-made structure in the Southern Hemisphere at 1,076 feet tall. It contains New Zealand's only revolving restaurant. It has become an iconic landmark in Auckland's skyline due to its height and unique design.

A town on the east coast of South Island, **Kaikoura** is located north of the Kaikoura Peninsula. Upwelling currents bring an abundance of marine life to the area from the Hikurangi Trench. The Kaikoura Range nearly come to the sea at the town, which contains a cottage made out of whalebone.

A 7.5-mile long glacier in Westland Tai Poutini National Park, **Franz Josef Glacier** is unique in descending from the Southern Alps to the greenery and lushness of a temperate rainforest. It is part of the Te Wahipounamu World Heritage Site. However, the glacier is retreating supposedly due to global warming. Jökulhlaups, or glacial outburst floods, have happened at the glacier.

The second largest lake of the North Island, **Lake Rotorua** is located in the Bay of Plenty Region. It was formed from the crater of a large volcano that last erupted 240,000 years ago. Due to the geothermal activity around the lake, it has a high sulfur content, giving it a yellow-greenish hue.

**Tongariro National Park** (see World Heritage Sites)

An area on the east coast near the Northland Peninsula, the **Bay of Islands** is one of the most popular fishing, sailing, and tourist destinations in New Zealand. In a study, the area was found to have the second bluest sky in the world after Rio de Janeiro. The largest town is Kerikeri, and Russell, the former capital of the country, is located at the end of a short peninsula.

A fjord in the southwestern part of South Island within Fiordland National Park, **Milford Sound** is part of the Te Wahipounamu World Heritage Site. Rudyard Kipling previously called it the eighth wonder of the world, and the sound is still the most popular tourist attraction in New Zealand. The Cleddau River flows into the sound. Hiking, canoeing, and other water sports are possible.

## World Heritage Sites

Comprising the five southernmost groups of the outlying islands of New Zealand, the **New Zealand Subantarctic Islands** lie near the southeast edge of the largely submerged continent known as Zealandia. These island groups are the Antipodes Islands, the Auckland Islands, the Bounty Islands, the Campbell Islands, and the Snares.

Containing some of the best representations of the original flora and fauna of Gondwana, **Te Wahipounamu** is Māori for "the place of greenstone". The site consists of four national parks, which as Aoraki/Mount Cook, Fiordland, Mount Aspiring, and Westland Tai Poutini National Parks.

The oldest national park in New Zealand, **Tongariro National Park** is located in the central part of North Island. Mounts Ruapehu, Ngauruhoe, and Tongariro are located in the center of the park, the fourth national park in world history. There are a number of Māori religious sites within the park, which contains a large part of the North Island Volcanic Plateau. It is the source of the Whanganui River.

# palau

# palau

## Political Geography

**Capital** Ngerulmud

**Five Largest States (Area)** Ngeremlengui, Koror, Aimeliik, Ngardmau, Ngatpang

**Five Largest States (Population)** Koror, Airai, Peleliu, Ngaraard, Ngarchelong

## Five Largest Cities

| City | State | Tourist Attractions | Body of Water |
|------|-------|---------------------|---------------|
| **Koror** | Koror | Belau National Museum, Palau Aquarium, Malakal Island, Ngatpang Waterfall | Pacific Ocean |
| **Meyuns** | Koror | N/A | Pacific Ocean |
| **Airai** | Airai | N/A | Pacific Ocean |
| **Kloulklubed** | Peleliu | N/A | Pacific Ocean |
| **Ulimang** | Ngaraard | N/A | Pacific Ocean |

## Physical Geography

**Relative Size** Slightly larger than the Seychelles or half the size of the Turks and Caicos Islands

**Highest Point** Located on the border of the states of Ngardmau and Ngaremlengui on the island of Babeldaob, Mount Ngerchelchuus is the highest point in Palau at 794 feet above sea level.

**Lowest Point** Pacific Ocean

## Islands

The largest island in Palau, **Babeldaob** is located in the western Caroline Islands. It is the second largest island in Micronesia after Guam, and it is home to thirty percent of Palau's population. It is the site of the capital, Ngerulmud, and it lies northeast of Koror Island. The Koror-Babeldaob Bridge links the two islands. Unlike most of the country's islands, Babeldaob is mountainous, containing the highest point, Mount Ngerchelchuus, and many mangrove forests. The island was first sighted by the Spanish expedition of Ruy López de Villalobos, and it was part of the Spanish East Indies from 1686 to 1899. As a result of the Spanish-American War, it was sold to Germany and administered by German New Guinea. 426 members of the Sokehs tribe of Pohnpei were banished to the island following the Sokehs Rebellion. The island was under Japanese control from World War I to 1947, when it was passed to the United States.

Also known as Oreor Island, **Koror Island** is the most populous island in Palau, home to seventy percent of the population and Koror, the former capital and largest city. It is connected by bridges to Ngerekebesang Island, the site of Meyuns, the second largest town; Malakal Island, the site of Koror's port, and Babeldaob, the country's largest island. The island was discovered by the Spanish, and it was the capital of the Japanese South Pacific Mandate from 1919 to 1947. Scuba diving and dolphin viewing are popular tourist draws.

Located six miles northeast of Angaur and 25 miles southwest of Koror, **Peleliu** has its capital at Kloulklubed, the fourth largest settlement in Palau. It was first sighted by the Spanish in 1543 and sold to Germany in 1899. The

Japanese took over in 1914. The island is best known for the Battle of Peleliu, which took place in 1944 and was controversial in the United States due to the high casualty rate. In 1947, it became part of the American Trust Territory of the Pacific Islands.

The northernmost state of Palau, **Kayangel** lies fifteen miles north of Koror and 22 miles north of Babeldaob. Its lagoon is home to a large diversity of coral species along with fish, dolphins, and sea turtles. Kayangel is the capital.

An island in the state of Koror, **Ngerekebesang Island** was where the office of Palau's president was located before the capital was moved to Ngerulmud. It is home to the town of Meyuns, the second largest settlement in Palau, connected to Koror by a causeway.

## Archipelagos

A widely scattered archipelago of tiny islands in the northwestern Pacific ocean north of New Guinea, the **Caroline Islands** are divided between Micronesia in the east and Palau in the west. Most of the islands are part of low, flat coral atolls. They were first sighted by Europeans in the early 16th century and claimed by the Spanish. After the Spanish-American War of 1898, the islands were sold to Germany in the German-Spanish treaty. They were invaded and occupied by Japan in both world wars, and after World War II, they became trust territories of the United States, with Micronesia gaining independence in 1986 and Palau in 1994.

**Palau** (the entire country is an archipelago)

**Rock Islands** (see World Heritage Sites)

A chain of several small islands spread across the Pacific Ocean 373 miles away from the rest of Palau, the **Southwest Islands** make up the states of Sonsorol and Hatohobei. Tobi Island, in Hatohobei, is the largest island of the chain, and its residents speak Tobian.

## Lakes

Located on Eil Malk, the main island of the Mecherchar Islands of the Rock Islands, **Jellyfish Lake** is known for its millions of golden jellyfish. It is one of the few permanently stratified marine lakes in the world, and it is connected to the sea via three tunnels. Snorkeling in the lake is a popular activity for tourists to Palau, although scuba diving is not allowed.

A lake on the island of Babeldaob in the state of Melekeok, **Lake Ngardok** is the largest natural freshwater lake in Micronesia. It is a refuge for the endangered saltwater crocodile, connected to the sea by the Ngerdorch River. The area is also home to Palau fruit doves, Palau fantails, Micronesian imperial pigeons, common moorhens, Pacific black ducks, and Palau flycatchers.

## Seas

Northeast of the Philippine Archipelago, northwest of Palau, Yap, and Ulithi of Micronesia, west of the Mariana Islands, southwest of Bonin and Iwo Jima, south of Honshu, Shikoku, and Kyushu, southeast of the Ryukyu Islands, and east of Taiwan, the **Philippine Sea** contains the Philippine Trench, the third lowest point on Earth. Island arcs extend above the ocean surface due to plate tectonics in the area.

# Economic Geography

**Currency** United States dollar

**Natural Resources** Forests, minerals, gold

**Agricultural Products** Coconuts, copra, cassava, sweet potatoes

**Port** Koror

## Historical Geography

**Former Capital** Koror (1994-2006)

**Empires** Spanish Empire (1885-1899), German Empire (1899-1914), Empire of Japan (1914-1947)

**Natives** Palauans

**Independence** From the United States, 1994

## Cultural Geography

**Language** Palauan, English (official), Japanese, Sonsorolese, Tobian (recognized regionally)

**Major Ethnic Groups** Palauan (72.5%), Filipino (16.3%), Chinese (1.6%), Vietnamese (1.6%), other Asian (3.4%), white (0.9%), Carolinian (1%), other Micronesian (2.4%), other (0.3%)

**Religion** Roman Catholic (49.4%), Protestant (21.3%), Modekngei (8.7%), Seventh-day Adventist (5.3%), Buddhist (1%), other (14.3%)

**Foods** Cassava, taro, yam, potato, fish, pork

## Destinations

### Tourist Attractions

**Jellyfish Lake** (see Lakes)

**Rock Islands** (see World Heritage Sites)

Located in Koror, the former capital and largest city of Palau, the **Belau National Museum** is the oldest museum in Micronesia, established in 1955. It was situated in the former Japanese weather bureau building, and the present building was funded by the Taiwanese government.

**Kayangel Atoll** (see Islands)

**Peleliu** (see Islands)

**Babeldaob** (see Islands)

## World Heritage Sites

A collection of 250 to 300 limestone or coral uprises between Koror Island and Peleliu, the **Rock Islands** are sparsely populated and famous for their beaches and blue lagoons. Ngeruktabel, Ulong, and Eil Malk are the largest islands in the group, which is home to manta rays, sharks, and dolphins. Jellyfish Lake on Eil Malk is famous for its golden jellyfish. Many of the islands are shaped like mushrooms due to erosion and the dense community of sponges, bivalves, chitons, snails, and urchins, which graze mostly on algae. The islands are also known as Chelbacheb.

# papua new guinea

# papua new guinea

## Political Geography

**Capital** Port Moresby

**Bordering Countries** Indonesia

**Five Largest Provinces (Area)** Western, East Sepik, West Sepik, Gulf, Morobe

**Five Largest Provinces (Population)** Morobe, Eastern Highlands, Southern Highlands, Madang, East Sepik

## Five Largest Cities

| City | Province | Tourist Attractions | Body of Water |
|------|----------|--------------------|--------------| 
| **Port Moresby** | National Capital District | N/A | Gulf of Papua |
| **Lae** | Morobe | N/A | Markham River, Huon Gulf |
| **Arawa** | Autonomous Region of Bougainville | N/A | Pacific Ocean |
| **Mount Hagen** | Western Highlands | N/A | N/A |
| **Madang** | Madang | N/A | Bismarck Sea |

# Physical Geography

**Relative Size** Twice the size of Laos or half the size of Nigeria or six times smaller than Argentina

**Highest Point** The highest point in Papua New Guinea, **Mount Wilhelm** is located in the Bismarck Range at 14,793 feet above sea level. It is claimed as the highest point in Oceania or Australia (the continent) on the condition that all of Indonesia is part of Asia. If the Indonesian region of West Papua is included in Oceania, Puncak Jaya is the highest point of the continent and region at 16,024 feet above sea level in the Sudirman Range of the Maoke Mountains. Mount Wilhelm is located at the tripoint of Madang, Simbu, and Western Highlands Provinces. It is the most accessible mountain to climb in the country.

**Lowest Point** Pacific Ocean

## Plateaus

Located in the Western and Southern Highlands Provinces of Papua New Guinea, the **Great Papua Plateau** is bounded by the Kikori and Strickland Rivers to the east and west, respectively. It is a karst plateau south of the Karius Range. A petroleum-transporting pipeline from the plateau to Daru, the capital of the Western Province near the mouth of the Fly River north of the Torres Strait, is being built.

## Volcanoes

One of the most active volcanoes in Papua New Guinea, **Ulawun** is one of the Decade Volcanoes. It is the highest point in the Bismarck Archipelago and New Britain at over 7,500 feet above sea level and releases 2% of the global total of $SO_2$ (sulfur dioxide) released into the atmosphere annually. It last erupted between 2013 and 2014.

The second highest point in Papua New Guinea after Mount Wilhelm, **Mount Giluwe** is the highest volcano on the Australian continent at 14,337 feet above sea level. Although located just six degrees south of the Equator, the volcano occasionally receives snow.

Also located on New Britain, **Tavurvur** largely destroyed the nearby town of Rabaul in 1994. A double eruption of Tavurvur and Vulcan, a nearby volcano, occurred in 1937, killing over 500 people. The volcano last erupted in 2014.

Located at the center of Bougainville, **Bagana** is the most active volcano in Papua New Guinea. It has continuously erupted since 2000 and has kept going for over a decade. It is located in the Emperor Range. Mount Balbi, the highest point on the island, is located just west of Bagana.

A stratovolcano in the Oro Province, **Mount Lamington** is located on the Bird's Tail (Papuan) Peninsula. Its eruption in 1951 remains the deadliest in Papua New Guinean history, killing nearly 3,000 people. The volcano caused pyroclastic flows, pumice dust, and sulfurous fumes.

## Mountain Ranges

A chain of mountain ranges and intermountain river valleys running from the northwest to the southeast of New Guinea, the **New Guinea Highlands** consist of ranges such as the Owen Stanley Range, the Albert Victor Mountains, the Sir Arthur Gordan Range, the Bismarck Range, the Star Mountains, and the Maoke Mountains, which contain Puncak Jaya, the highest point of New Guinea. Some of the peaks are capped in ice even though New Guinea is located just south of the Equator.

Located in southeastern Papua New Guinea on the Bird's Tail (Papuan) Peninsula, the **Owen Stanley** Range is located in the Central and Oro Provinces. Mount Victoria is the highest point in the range at 13,248 feet above sea level.

Located in the central highlands of Papua New Guinea, the **Bismarck Range** was named after the German Chancellor Otto von Bismarck when the region was part of Germany. The highest point is Mount Wilhelm, the highest point in the country, at 14,793 feet above sea level. It has an alpine tundra landscape even though the surrounding area has a tropical climate. The range is the source of the Ramu River.

Located on the Huon Peninsula in Morobe Province in the northeastern part of Papua New Guinea, the **Saruwaged Range** merges into the Finisterre Range to the west and forms a barrier between the Ramu and Markham river valleys and the Vitiaz Strait, which separates New Guinea from Umboi Island.

## Islands

The largest island in the Malay Archipelago, **New Guinea** is the world's second largest island after Greenland. It is divided between Indonesia and Papua New Guinea. It is included as part of Melanesia, which is why Puncak Jaya in Indonesia is considered the highest point in Oceania. The largest city is Jayapura in Indonesia. The Arafura Sea, Coral Sea, and Torres Strait separated the island from Australia. The Bismarck Sea is located north of New Britain and Papua New Guinea while the Solomon Sea is located south of New Britain and northwest of the Solomon Islands. The Bird's Head (Doberai) Peninsula is located in the northwest while the Bird's Tail (Papuan) Peninsula is located in the southeast. The New Guinea Highlands dominate the geography of the island. The Sepik River is the world's longest river on an island.

The largest island in the Bismarck Archipelago, **New Britain** is separated from New Guinea by the Dampier and Vitiaz Straits and from New Ireland by Saint George's Channel. The Dampier Strait is located between New Britain and Umboi Island while the Vitiaz Strait separates Umboi Island from the Huon Peninsula. The island is about the size of Taiwan. Rabaul, Kokopo, and Kimbe are the main towns. It was formerly known as Neupommern, or "New

Pomerania", when it was part of German New Guinea. Ulawun, Tavurvur, and Vulcan are major volcanoes on the island.

Although not located in the Solomon Islands, **Bougainville** is the largest island in the Solomon Islands archipelago. Bougainville declared independence in 1975 and 1990, giving the island autonomy after peace talks in 1997. Mount Bagana is a major volcano on the island. Mount Balbi is the highest point.

Located northeast of New Britain, **New Ireland** is part of the Bismarck Archipelago. It is separated from New Britain by Saint George's Channel. When part of German New Guinea, the island was known as Neumecklenberg, or "New Mecklenburg".

## Archipelagos

The world's largest archipelago by area, the **Malay Archipelago** contains portions or all of Brunei, East Timor, Indonesia, Malaysia, the Philippines, and Singapore (and Papua New Guinea, depending on the definition). The archipelago is also the fourth largest by number of islands in the world.

Consisting mainly of volcanic islands, the **Bismarck Archipelago** surrounds the Bismarck Sea with New Guinea. New Britain and New Ireland are the main islands in the archipelago. The 1888 eruption of Ritter Island triggered a megatsunami. The archipelago sits upon the Manus and North and South Bismarck Plates.

Located near the eastern tip of New Guinea, the **D'entrecasteaux Islands** are located in the Solomon Sea in Milne Bay Province. Ferguson (Moratau) Island is the largest of the three principal islands, the other being Goodenough (Nidula) and Normanby (Duau) Islands. The Ward Hunt Strait separates New Guinea from Goodenough Island.

Also located in the Milne Bay Province, the **Louisiade Archipelago** is located between the Solomon Sea to the north and the Coral Sea to the south.

Vanatinai Island is the largest island by area while Misima Island is the most populous.

The archipelago of the **Solomon Islands** contains most of the country of the Solomon Islands and Bougainville in Papua New Guinea and its surrounding islands. Bougainville is the largest island in the archipelago; Guadalcanal is the second largest and the largest in the country of the Solomon Islands. They are a subregion of Melanesia, itself a subregion of Oceania.

| River | Source | Mouth | Cities (if any) |
|---|---|---|---|
| **Sepik** | Victor Emanuel Range (Papua New Guinea) | Bismarck Sea (Papua New Guinea) | N/A |
| **Fly** | Victor Emanuel Range (Papua New Guinea) | Gulf of Papua (Papua New Guinea) | N/A |
| **Ramu** | Kratke Range (Papua New Guinea) | Bismarck Sea (Papua New Guinea) | N/A |
| **Purari** | Confluence of Tua and Pio Rivers (Papua New Guinea) | Gulf of Papua (Papua New Guinea) | N/A |
| **Kikori** | Papua New Guinea | Gulf of Papua (Papua New Guinea) | Kikori (Papua New Guinea) |

# Lakes

Located in the Western Province, **Lake Murray** is the largest lake in Papua New Guinea. The Herbert River flows out of the lake into the Strickland River, which flows into the Fly River, which flows into the Gulf of Papua. A creature known as "Murray" is said to live in the lake and is supposed to resemble a T-rex.

Located in the Southern Highlands Province, **Lake Kutubu** is the second largest lake in Papua New Guinea after Lake Murray. The country's first oilfield development project took place at the lake, which is located fifty kilometers south of Mendi, the provincial capital. It is one of the few lakes in the country in a depression in the interior highlands.

# Gulfs

An inlet of the Coral Sea, the **Gulf of Papua** is the mouth of many of New Guinea's largest rivers, such as the Fly, Kikori, Purari, and Turama Rivers. Port Moresby, the capital of Papua New Guinea, is located on the gulf.

An inlet of the Solomon Sea, the **Huon Gulf** is bordered by the Huon Peninsula to the north. Lae, the capital of the Morobe Province, is located on the northern coast of the gulf. This part of the gulf is known as Markham Bay because it is the mouth of the Markham River.

# Seas

Located north of the Gulf of Carpentaria, east of the Timor Sea, southeast of the Banda and Ceram Seas, south of New Guinea, and west of the Torres Strait which connects it to the Coral Sea, the **Arafura Sea** is bordered by Australia, Indonesia, and Papua New Guinea. It is home to one of the richest marine fisheries in the world and has a lot of potential in terms of exports.

Surrounded by New Guinea to the west and the Bismarck Archipelago to the east, the **Bismarck Sea** is linked to the Solomon Sea by the Dampier and

Vitiaz Straits. Like the Bismarck Archipelago, it was named after German chancellor Otto von Bismarck. Minerals such as sulfides, copper, zinc, silver, and gold have been found in the sea. The rights to mine these minerals are owned by Papua New Guinea under international law.

Bordered by Australia, New Caledonia (France), Papua New Guinea, the Solomon Islands, and Vanuatu, the **Coral Sea** contains the world's largest reef system, the Great Barrier Reef (a UNESCO World Heritage Site). It is a popular tourist attraction for birds and aquatic life. It borders the Solomon Sea to the north, the Pacific Ocean to the east, Queensland to the west, the Tasman Sea to the south, and the Torres Strait (which connects it to the Arafura Sea) in the northwest.

Located north of the Coral Sea and southeast of the Bismarck Sea (to which it is connected by the Dampier and Vitiaz Straits), the **Solomon Sea** was famous for the many battles fought there in World War II. It is bordered by Papua New Guinea and the Solomon Islands.

## Straits

Separating New Britain from Umboi Island, the **Dampier Strait** links the Bismarck Sea in the north to the Solomon Sea in the south. In 1942, Japanese forces landed two battalions at Lae and Salamaua on the Huon Gulf, which gave them control of the strait and the nearby Vitiaz Strait. However, the area was occupied by American forces in 1944.

Located between the Western Province of Papua New Guinea and Australia's Cape York Peninsula in Queensland, the **Torres Strait** is 93 miles wide at its narrowest width. It links the Arafura Sea in the west to the Coral Sea in the east. The Endeavour Strait separates Prince of Wales (Muralug) Island and mainland Australia. The strait allows illegal immigrants from Papua New Guinea to enter Australia.

Separating New Guinea from Umboi Island, the **Vitiaz Strait** links the Bismarck Sea in the north to the Solomon Sea in the south. In 1942, Japanese forces landed two battalions at Lae and Salamaua on the Huon Gulf, which gave them control of the strait and the nearby Dampier Strait. However, the area was occupied by American forces in 1944.

## Peninsulas

Making up the southeastern portion of the island of New Guinea, the **Papuan Peninsula** is situated southeast of Lae. It consists mainly of the Owen Stanley Range and contains its highest peak, Mount Victoria. Port Moresby, the capital and largest city of Papua New Guinea, is located on the southern coast of the peninsula, which is also known as the Bird's Tail Peninsula.

## Economic Geography

**Currency** Papua New Guinean kina

**Natural Resources** Gold, copper, silver, natural gas, timber, oil, fisheries

**Agricultural Products** Coffee, cocoa, copra, tea, sugar, yams

**Ports** Port Moresby (largest port), Lae

## Historical Geography

**Former Names** Papua, New Guinea, British New Guinea, German New Guinea, Territory of Papua, Territory of New Guinea, Territory of Papua and New Guinea

**Empires** German Empire (1884-1919), British Empire (1884-1975), Empire of Japan (1941-1945)

**Natives** Papuans, Austronesians

**Independence** From Australia, 1975

# Cultural Geography

**Language** Hiri Motu, Tok Pisin, English (official)

**Major Ethnic Groups** Papuans, Austronesians, Chinese, Europeans, Australians, Filipinos, Polynesians, Micronesians, other

**Religion** Roman Catholic (27%), Evangelical Lutheran Church of Papua New Guinea (19.5%), United Church in Papua New Guinea and the Solomon Islands (11.5%), Seventh-day Adventists (10%), Pentecostal (8.6%), Evangelical (5.2%), Anglican Church of Papua New Guinea (3.2%), Baptist (2.5%), Church of Christ (0.4%), other Christian (8.9%), Bahá'í (0.3%), indigenous and other (2.9%)

**Foods** Sago

# Destinations

## Tourist Attractions

The longest river on the island of New Guinea and the third largest by volume (after the Fly in Papua New Guinea and the Mamberamo, the largest by volume in all of Indonesia), the **Sepik River** forms possibly the largest uncontaminated freshwater wetland system in the Asia-Pacific region. It originates in the Victor Emanuel Range of the Star Mountains in the central highlands of Papua New Guinea and flows into the Bismarck Sea. It is notable for having no delta whatsoever, unlike many other large rivers. The Chambri Lakes are located in the Sepik floodplain.

A popular trekking destination in the Owen Stanley Range, the **Kokoda Track** runs from Owens Corner, 31 miles east of Port Moresby, to the village of Kokoda. Hot, humid days, intensely cold nights, torrential rainfall, and malaria make it a challenging trek. It is growing in popularity and is now one of the most popular tourist attractions in Papua New Guinea.

**Mount Wilhelm** (see Highest Point)

**Owen Stanley Range** (see Mountain Ranges)

Probably the best-known tribal gathering and cultural event in Papua New Guinea, the **Goroka Show** is held in the town of Goroka, the capital of the Eastern Highlands Provinces. It is known as a sing-sing, or a gathering of tribes or villages to showcase culture, dance, and music. Similar shows are now being organized in Mount Hagen and other cities around Papua New Guinea.

**Tavurvur** (see Volcanoes)

Located in Milne Bay Province in southeastern Papua New Guinea, **Milne Bay** was the site of the Battle of Milne Bay in World War II. It was part of the Huon Peninsula campaign, which resulted in an Allied victory by Australia and the United States.

**Mount Giluwe** (see Volcanoes)

A rough overland track in Morobe Province, the **Black Cat Track** runs from the village of Salamaua on the coast of the Huon Gulf to the town of Wau. The trail originates from the 1920s and 30s as a trail for prospectors looking for gold.

Originating just south of Mount Karimui, the **Purari River** flows into the Gulf of Papua. It is the fourth longest river in Papua New Guinea and has brown water due to the silt washed down from the mountains.

Having Tavurvur as one of its subvents, the **Rabaul Caldera** is located on the tip of the Gazelle Peninsula on New Britain. In 1937, a simultaneous eruption of Tavurvur and nearby Vulcan occurred.

A foot track crossing the western end of the Owen Stanley Range, the **Bulldog Track** is located 100 kilometers west of the famous Kokoda Track and crosses some of the most rugged and isolated terrain in the world.

**Bismarck Range** (see Mountain Ranges)

A subvent of the Rabaul caldera, **Vulcan** is a pumice cone that forced the temporary abandonment of the city of Rabaul. This led to the capital of East New Britain Province becoming Kokopo. The cone last erupted from 1994 to 1995.

## World Heritage Sites

Located in the Kuk Swamp in the Wahgi Valley, the **Kuk Early Agricultural Site** contains evidence for early agricultural drainage systems created about 9,000 years ago. Crops such as taro, bananas, and sugarcane were grown at the site. It is one of the earliest sites for the development of agriculture in the world.

# samoa

# samoa

## Political Geography

**Capital** Apia

**Five Largest Districts (Area)** Palauli, Tuamasaga, Atua, Gaga'ifomauga, Fa'asaleleaga

**Five Largest Districts (Population)** Tuamasaga, Atua, A'ana, Fa'asaleleaga, Palauli

## Five Largest Cities

| City | District | Tourist Attractions | Body of Water |
|------|----------|---------------------|---------------|
| Apia | Tuamasaga | Robert Louis Stevenson Museum, Piula Cave Pool, Mount Vaea | Vaisigano River, Pacific Ocean |
| Asau | Vaisigano | N/A | Pacific Ocean |
| Mulifanua | Aiga-i-le-Tai | N/A | Apolima Strait |
| Malie | Tuamasaga | N/A | Pacific Ocean |
| Fasito'o Uta | A'ana | N/A | Pacific Ocean |

## Volcanoes

**Savai'i** (see Islands)

**Upolu** (see Islands)

# Islands

The largest and highest island in Samoa and the Samoan Islands, **Savai'i** is the fifth largest island in Polynesia after the two main islands of New Zealand and the Hawaiian islands of Hawaii and Maui. It is the largest shield volcano in the South Pacific, home to 82 bird species and more native fern and butterfly species than New Zealand. The Central Savai'i Rainforest is the largest continuous patch of rainforest in Polynesia. The island lies northwest of Upolu, separated from it by the Apolima Strait. Fa'a Samoa, the traditional Samoan culture and way of life, is much stronger on the island than in Upolu due to the lack of development on the island, which is only home to 24 percent of Samoa's population. Salelologa is the main port and township on the island, which has excellent surfing.

The second largest and most populous island of the Samoan Islands, **Upolu** was formed by a massive basaltic shield volcano rising from the seafloor of the Pacific Ocean. It is home to Samoa's capital and largest city, Apia, as well as its most important airport, Faleolo International Airport. A spider the size of a period on a printed page can be found on the island.

# Archipelagos

A Polynesian archipelago in the south-central Pacific Ocean, the **Samoan Islands** consist of the country of Samoa and the American unincorporated territory of American Samoa. The region shares the Samoan language, fa'a Samoa (the Samoan way), and fa'amatai (a form of governance). Upolu is the most populous island in the group while Savai'i is the largest. Apia, the capital of Samoa, is the largest city, while the largest American Samoan settlement is Tafuna, on Tutuila. Silisili on Savai'i is the highest point in the archipelago, while Lata Mountain is the highest American Samoan point.

## Straits

A strait about eight miles wide separating the islands of Savai'i and Upolu, the **Apolima Strait** contains the islands of Manono, Apolima, and Nu'ulopa. Manono is the largest island in the strait and the third most populous island in Samoa.

# Economic Geography

**Currency** Samoan tālā

**Natural Resources** Hardwood forests, fish, hydropower

**Agricultural Products** Coconuts, bananas, taro, yams, coffee, cocoa

**Ports** Apia (largest port), Salelologa

# Historical Geography

**Former Name** Western Samoa

**Historic City** Apia (est. 1850s)

**Empires** German Empire (1899-1919)

**Natives** Samoans

**Independence** From New Zealand, 1962

# Cultural Geography

**Language** Samoan, English (official)

**Major Ethnic Groups** Samoan (92.6%), Euronesian (7%), European (0.4%), East Asian (0.1%)

**Religion** Christian Congregational Church of Samoa (31.8%), Roman Catholic (19.4%), Mormon (15.1%), Methodist (13.7%), Assemblies of God (8%), Seventh-Day Adventist (3.9%), other (8.1%)

**Foods** Coconut, pork, rice, taro, coconut, seaweed, crayfish

# Destinations

## National Parks

**Lake Lanoto'o National Park** (no information available)

**Pupu Pu'e National Park** (no information available)

## Tourist Attractions

A natural feature in the district of Palauli in the southern part of Savai'i, the **Alofaaga Blowholes** were created by lava flows. The area is unfenced and surrounded by dangerous, wet, and slippery rocks. A track along the coast leads to the ancient village of Fagaloa.

A village in the district of Atua in the eastern part of the island of Upolu, **Lalomanu** is the site of one of the most popular beaches in Samoa. It has rich coral lagoons and one of the best views in the country, and the uninhabited island of Nu'utele, the largest of the Aleipata Islands, lies just off the coast.

A natural freshwater pool by the sea in the district of Atua on the island of Upolu, the **Piula Cave Pool** was formed by a natural spring flowing out of a cave into the sea. It lies near the Piula Theological College, a Methodist training institution established in 1868.

A village in the district of Vaisigano on the northwestern end of the island of Savai'i, **Falealupo** is mentioned in several different Samoan myths and legends. It includes large tracts of lowland rainforest, which was protected by Paul Alan Cox, an American ethnobotanist.

A summit overlooking Apia, the capital and largest city of Samoa on the island of Upolu, **Mount Vaea** is well-known as the burial place of Robert Louis Stevenson, who lived the last four years of his life in the country, and his wife, Fanny Stevenson.

An active volcano on the island of Savai'i, **Mount Matavanu** last erupted from 1905 to 1911. Due to the destruction of some villages by the volcano, they were relocated inland. The lava fields produced by the eruption can still be seen today.

# solomon islands

# solomon islands

## Political Geography

**Capital** Honiara

**Five Largest Provinces (Area)** Western, Guadalcanal, Malaita, Isabel, Choiseul

**Five Largest Provinces (Population)** Malaita, Guadalcanal, Western, Capital Territory, Makira-Ulawa

## Five Largest Cities

| City | District | Tourist Attractions | Body of Water |
|------|----------|---------------------|---------------|
| Honiara | Capital Territory | N/A | Matanikau River, Lunga River, Pacific Ocean |
| Gizo | Western | N/A | Pacific Ocean |
| Auki | Malaita | N/A | Langa Langa Lagoon |
| Noro | Western | N/A | Pacific Ocean |
| Buala | Isabel | N/A | Pacific Ocean |

## Physical Geography

**Relative Size** About the size of Albania or twice the size of Connecticut

**Highest Point** Located on Guadalcanal east of Mount Makarakomburu, the second highest point, **Mount Popomanaseu** is the highest point of the Solomon Islands and the entire South Pacific (excluding New Guinea and its surrounding islands). Its elevation is 7,661 feet above sea level.

**Lowest Point** Pacific Ocean

# Volcanoes

One of the most active submarine volcanoes in the southwestern Pacific Ocean, **Kavachi** is located south of Vangunu Island. It was named after a sea god of the people of the New Georgia Group and last erupted in 2014.

A conical stratovolcano that forms an island north of Nendo, the largest of the Santa Cruz Islands, **Tinakula** is uninhabited. It last erupted in 2007.

An active volcano on Simbo Island, **Ove** last erupted in 1910. It was hit by a massive earthquake and tsunami in 2007.

A stratovolcano that forms an island off the western tip of Guadalcanal, **Savo** last erupted in 1847.

# Islands

Named after Guadalcanal, a village in Spain where a member of Álvaro de Mendaña's expedition (which discovered Guadalcanal) was born, **Guadalcanal** is the largest island in the Solomon Islands. It was important in World War II as a site of large battles between American and Japanese troops; the Americans won in the end. The island is natively known as Isatabu.

The most populous island of the Solomon Islands, **Malaita** is separated from South Malaita Island by the narrow Maramasike Passage. The largest city and the capital of the Malaita Province is Auki, on the northern shore of the Langa Langa Lagoon.

The largest island of the Makira-Ulawa Province, **Makira** has its largest settlement at Kirakira, the capital of the province. The island was formerly known as San Cristóbal.

The longest island in the Solomon Islands, **Santa Isabel** is part of the Isabel province, which has its capital and largest settlement at Buala. The highest point is Mount Sasari.

Located in the Choiseul Province, **Choiseul** is natively known as Lauru. The capital of Choiseul Province is the town of Taro.

The largest island of the New Georgia Group, **New Georgia** is located in the Western Province. However, the capital of the Western Province, Gizo, is situated on Ghizo Island.

## Archipelagos

The archipelago of the **Solomon Islands** contains most of the country of the Solomon Islands and Bougainville in Papua New Guinea and its surrounding islands. Bougainville is the largest island in the archipelago; Guadalcanal is the second largest and the largest in the country of the Solomon Islands. They are a subregion of Melanesia, itself a subregion of Oceania.

## Rivers

| River | Source | Mouth | Cities (if any) |
|---|---|---|---|
| **Lunga** | Guadalcanal | Savo Sound | Honiara |
| **Matanikau** | Guadalcanal | Savo Sound | Honiara |
| **Tenaru** | Guadalcanal | Savo Sound | N/A |

# Seas

Bordered by Australia, New Caledonia (France), Papua New Guinea, the Solomon Islands, and Vanuatu, the **Coral Sea** contains the world's largest reef system, the Great Barrier Reef (a UNESCO World Heritage Site). It is a popular tourist attraction for birds and aquatic life. It borders the Solomon Sea to the north, the Pacific Ocean to the east, Queensland to the west, the Tasman Sea to the south, and the Torres Strait (which connects it to the Arafura Sea) in the northwest.

Located north of the Coral Sea and southeast of the Bismarck Sea, the **Solomon Sea** was famous for the many battles fought there in World War II. It is bordered by Papua New Guinea and the Solomon Islands.

## Economic Geography

**Currency** Solomon Islands dollar

**Natural Resources** Fish, forests, gold, bauxite, phosphates, lead, zinc, nickel

**Agricultural Products** Cocoa, coconuts, palm kernels, rice, potatoes, vegetables, fruit, cattle, pigs, fish, timber

**Port** Honiara

## Historical Geography

**Former Capital** Tulagi (1896-1942)

**Empires** Hawaiian Empire (19th century), German Empire (1886-1899), British Empire (1899-1978), Empire of Japan (1942-1945)

**Natives** Melanesians

**Independence** From the United Kingdom, 1978

# Cultural Geography

**Language** English (official), Solomons Pijin (lingua franca)

**Major Ethnic Groups** Melanesian (94.5%), Polynesian (3%), Micronesian (1.2%), other (1.3%)

**Religion** Anglican Church of Melanesia (35%), Roman Catholic (19%), South Seas Evangelical Church (17%), United Church in Papua New Guinea and the Solomon Islands (11%), Seventh-day Adventist (10%), aboriginal beliefs (5%), other (3%)

**Foods** Coconuts, palm kernels, rice, potatoes, vegetables, fruit, fish

# Destinations

## Tourist Attractions

A saltwater lagoon north of Vangunu Island, the **Marovo Lagoon** is protected by a double barrier reef system. It is a popular destination for diving in the New Georgia Islands.

A double-sided waterfall, the **Mataniko Falls** drop into a cave full of stalagmites. During World War II, this cave was a hide-out for Japanese soldiers trying to avoid capture by the Americans.

A waterfall on the Chea River, **Tenaru Falls** is located in the rainforest of Guadalcanal.

**Rennell Island** (see World Heritage Sites)

Locally known as Kasolo Island, **Kennedy Island** was named after John F. Kennedy due to his escape to this island when his craft, PT-109, was wrecked by the Japanese destroyer Amagiri. The island is fifteen minutes from Gizo, the capital of the Western Province.

Also known as Mushroom Island, **Tomba Tuni** is a great site for diving.

An exciting cave dive is possible at the **Cave of the Kastom Shark**. It is a good place to see pygmy seahorses.

Located in the Vona Vona Lagoon, **Lola Island** is sacred to the people who live there.

## World Heritage Sites

The main island of the Rennell and Bellona Province, **Rennell Island** is the world's second largest raised coral atoll. It contains Lake Tegano, the largest lake in the islands of the South Pacific. They contain many different species.

# tonga

# tonga

## Political Geography

**Sobriquet** Friendly Islands

**Capital** Nuku'alofa

**Five Largest Divisions (Area)** Tongatapu, Vava'u, Ha'apai, 'Eua, Niuas

**Five Largest Divisions (Population)** Tongatapu, Vava'u, Ha'apai, 'Eua, Niuas

## Five Largest Cities

| City | Division | Tourist Attractions | Body of Water |
| --- | --- | --- | --- |
| **Nuku'alofa** | Tongatapu | Tonga National Museum | Pacific Ocean |
| **Neiafu** | Vava'u | 'Ene'io Botanical Garden | Pacific Ocean |
| **Haveluloto** | Tongatapu | N/A | Pacific Ocean |
| **Vaini** | Tongatapu | N/A | Pacific Ocean |
| **Pangai** | Ha'apai | N/A | Pacific Ocean |

## Physical Geography

**Relative Size** About the size of Dominica or Singapore

**Highest Point** Unnamed location on Kao Island (3,379 feet above sea level)

**Lowest Point** Pacific Ocean

## Volcanoes

Located 19 miles south-southeast of Fonuafo'ou Island, **Hunga Tonga-Hunga Ha'apai** is part of the highly active Tonga-Kermadec Islands volcanic arc. From December 2014 to January 2015, the eruption of this volcano created a new island which later merged with an existing island.

A temporary island built by a submarine volcano, the 2006 eruption of **Home Reef** caused floating pumice to be swept across the ocean to Fiji. There are several small hot crater lakes on the island.

## Islands

The main island of Tonga, **Tongatapu** is home to the national capital, Nuku'alofa. The island contains 70.5% of the national population and is the center of government and the seat of the monarchy.

Home to the 'Ene'io Botanical Garden, the only botanical garden in Tonga, **Vava'** is the second largest island in Tonga, both by area and population. Neiafu is the capital and largest city.

## Archipelagos

**Tonga** (the entire country is an archipelago)

# Economic Geography

**Currency** Tonga pa'anga

**Natural Resources** Fish, arable land

**Agricultural Products** Coconuts, vanilla beans, bananas

**Port** Nuku'alofa

# Historical Geography

**Empires** Tu'i Tonga Empire (950s-1865), British Empire (1900-1970)

**Natives** Tongans

**Independence** End of British protectorate, 1970

# Cultural Geography

**Language** Tongan, English (official)

**Major Ethnic Groups** Tongan (98%), mixed Tongans (1.5%), other (0.5%)

**Religion** Free Wesleyan and Methodist (36%), Mormon (18%), Roman Catholic (15%), Free Church of Tonga (12%), other (19%)

**Foods** Coconuts, fish, bananas

# Destinations

## Tourist Attractions

A stone trilithon in northern Tongatapu, **Ha'amonga 'A Maui** was built in the early 13th century. It is quoted as being similar to Stonehenge but is actually much simpler.

The first and only botanical garden in Tonga, the **'Ene'io Botanical Garden** is located on Vava'u Island near the city of Neiafu. It contains many native and exotic plant species.

A caldera on Tofua Island, **Tofua** is part of the Ha'apai island group. It has a neighboring island, Kao Island.

A natural land bridge on Tongatapu, **Hufangalupe** was formed by the collapse of the roof of a sea cave on the southeastern coast of the island. "Hufangalupe" means "pigeon's gate" in Tongan.

# tuvalu

# tuvalu

## Political Geography

**Capital** Funafuti

**Eight Largest Districts (Area)** Vaitupu, Nanumea, Nanumanga, Nukufetau, Niutao, Nui, Funafuti, Nukulaelae

**Eight Largest Districts (Population)** Funafuti, Vaitupu, Niutao, Nanumea, Nanumanga, Nukufetau, Nui, Nukulaelae

## Five Largest Cities

| City | District | Tourist Attractions | Body of Water |
|------|----------|--------------------|---------------|
| **Funafuti** | Funafuti | N/A | Pacific Ocean |
| **Asau** | Vaitupu | N/A | Pacific Ocean |
| **Savave** | Nukufetau | N/A | Pacific Ocean |
| **Vaiaku** | Funafuti | N/A | Pacific Ocean |
| **Tanrake** | Nui | N/A | Pacific Ocean |

## Physical Geography

**Relative Size** Slightly larger than Nauru or half the size of Bermuda

**Highest Point** Unnamed location on Niulakita (fifteen feet above sea level)

**Lowest Point** Pacific Ocean

## Islands and Atolls

The atoll on which the capital of Tuvalu is located, **Funafuti** contains over half the country's population. It encircles the largest lagoon in Tuvalu, and the largest island is Fongafale. The ancestor of the island's people is described as being from Samoa. Fongafale is the site of Funafuti International Airport, the Parliament of Tuvalu, and the Princess Margaret Hospital, the only hospital in the country. The Funafuti Conservation Area encompasses six of the atoll's islets.

The northwesternmost atoll in Tuvalu, **Nanumea** lies just south of the Gilbert Islands. The Nanumea Conservation Area covers part of the central lagoon. Nanumea and Lakea are the two largest islands of the atoll, whose residents speak a dialect of Tuvaluan.

An atoll of Tuvalu, **Nui** consists of at least 21 islets, the largest and southeasternmost of which is Fenua Tapu. Since the ancestors of the atoll's residents came from Samoa and the Gilbert Islands, many people speak Gilbertese and Tuvaluan. Cyclone Pam destroyed ninety percent of the atoll's crops in 2015.

An atoll of Tuvalu, **Nukufetau** consists of at least 33 islets. The most populous island of the atoll is Savave, and the largest island is Motulalo. Tongans are said to be the first inhabitants of the atoll, which was severely affected by Cyclone Pam in 2015.

An atoll of Tuvalu, **Nukulaelae** consists of at least fifteen islets. Its largest settlement is Pepesala on Fangaua, the largest islet of the atoll. It is said that there were no people on the island when it was discovered. The atoll was claimed by the United States under the Guano Islands Act from the 19th century to 1983.

The largest atoll of Tuvalu, **Vaitupu** is said to have first been inhabited by a Samoan in the 16th or 17th century. The population mostly resides in the village of Asau. The atoll consists of at least nine islets, and it was severely affected by Cyclone Ofa in 1990 and Cyclone Pam in 2015.

A reef island of Tuvalu, **Nanumanga** contains three lagoons, mangrove trees, native broadleaf forest, and coconut palms. It was severely affected by Cyclone Pam in 2015. In 1986, the Caves of Nanumanga were discovered off the northern shore of the atoll, suggesting the use of fire by ancient occupants.

The southernmost reef island of Tuvalu, **Niulakita** is said to have been discovered by travelers from Nui. It was first sighted by the Spanish navigator Álvaro de Mendaña de Neira in 1595, and it was claimed by the United States under the Guano Islands Act from 1856 to 1983.

A reef island in northern Tuvalu, **Niutao** contains two ponds or lagoons. It was severely affected by Cyclone Pam in 2015, and residents grown breadfruit, coconuts, and pandanus. The islanders believe that their ancestors came from Samoa in the 12th or 13th century.

## Archipelagos

**Tuvalu** (the entire country is an archipelago)

## Economic Geography

**Currency** Tuvaluan dollar, Australian dollar

**Natural Resources** Fish

**Agricultural Products** Coconuts, swamp taro, bananas, breadfruit, pandanus, sugarcane

**Port** Funafuti

# Historical Geography

**Former Name** Ellice Islands

**Empires** British Empire (1892-1978)

**Natives** Polynesians

**Independence** From the United Kingdom, 1978

# Cultural Geography

**Language** Tuvaluan, English (official)

**Major Ethnic Groups** Polynesian (96%), Micronesian (4%)

**Religion** Congregational Christian Church of Tuvalu (97%), Seventh-day Adventist (1.4%), Bahá'í (1%), Ahmadiyya Muslim (0.4%), other (1.6%)

**Foods** Pulaka, bananas, breadfruit, coconuts, seafood, pork

# Destinations

## Tourist Attractions

A marine conservation area on the western side of the atoll of Funafuti, the **Funafuti Conservation Area** is home to many species of fish, corals, algae, and invertebrates. It is a nesting site for the green sea turtle, and the islet of Fualopa hosts a breeding colony of black noddies. The area was established in 1999, and it consists of the islets of Tepuka Vili Vili, Fualopa, Fuafatu, Vasafua, Fuagea, and Tefala. Coconut crabs live on the islets, and hawksbill and leatherback sea turtles live nearby. Gray reef sharks, blacktip reef sharks, whitetip reef sharks, lemon sharks, manta rays, and spotted eagle rays can also be found in the area, along with many other species.

# vanuatu

# vanuatu

## Political Geography

**Capital** Port Vila

**Six Largest Provinces (Area)** Sanma, Malampa, Tafea, Shefa, Penama, Torba

**Six Largest Provinces (Population)** Shefa, Sanma, Malampa, Tafea, Penama, Torba

## Five Largest Cities

| City | Province | Tourist Attractions | Body of Water |
|------|----------|---------------------|---------------|
| **Port Vila** | Shefa | Vanuatu Cultural Center, National Museum of Vanuatu, Wet N Wild Zorbing, Blokart Vanuatu, Hideaway Island Resort, Volcanic Earth Day Spa, Bluewater Island Resort Aquarium, Tanna Coffee Roasting Factory | Pacific Ocean |
| **Luganville** | Sanma | Lysepsep Culture Park | Pacific Ocean |
| **Port Olry** | Sanma | N/A | Pacific Ocean |
| **Isangel** | Tafea | N/A | Pacific Ocean |

| City | Province | Tourist Attractions | Body of Water |
|------|----------|---------------------|---------------|
| **Norsup** | Malampa | N/A | Pacific Ocean |

## Physical Geography

**Relative Size** About twice the size of Palestine or half the size of New Hampshire

**Highest Point** Located on the isolated western coast of Espiritu Santo, Mount Tabwemasana is the highest point of Vanuatu at 6,165 feet above sea level and one of the highest mountains in the Pacific. Very few tourists climb the peak each year due to the difficulty of reaching the mountain and climbing it.

**Lowest Point** Pacific Ocean

## Volcanoes

An active volcano on Tanna Island, **Mount Yasur** is a sacred area for the John Frum cargo cult. It is considered the most accessible volcano in the world and is very important to Vanuatu's tourism industry.

## Islands

The largest island in Vanuatu, **Espiritu Santo** contains Mount Tabwemasana, the highest point of the country. Luganville, on the southeastern coast, is the second largest settlement in the country and the provincial capital of the Sanma Provinces. The island is home to all of the country's endemic birds.

The second largest island in Vanuatu, **Malakula** is separated from Espiritu Santo and Malo by the Bougainville Strait. The Maskelynes Islands are to the southeast of the island, which speaks nearly thirty different languages. The island is part of Malampa Province.

The most populous island of Vanuatu, **Efate** contains the national capital, Port Vila. The highest point is Mount McDonald. The island is part of the Shefa Province and is also known as Île Vate. Port Vila is the hub of tourism in the country.

The fourth largest island in Vanuatu, **Erromango** is the largest island of Tafea Province, the southernmost of Vanuatu's provinces. Dense evergreen forest covers part of the island while the rest is occupied by a combination of grassland and woodland. The island was historically linguistically diverse.

A volcanic island in the Malampa Province, **Ambrym** is the fifth largest island of Vanuatu. Most of the island is covered by thick jungle. Mount Benbow, a large basaltic volcano, has had destructive eruptions. Coconut plantations occupy three corners of the island.

## Archipelagos

Forming the Torba Province with the Torres Islands, the **Banks Islands** contain Gaua and Vanua Lava, two of the largest islands of Vanuatu. Although the islands have less than 10,000 people, fifteen different languages are spoken in the archipelago.

Located 190 miles east of New Caledonia, the **Matthew and Hunter Islands** consist of two uninhabited volcanic islands. During the colonization of the Pacific by Britain and France, the islands were left unclaimed. Vanuatu claims sovereignty over the islands although they are administered and claimed by New Caledonia, a French overseas collectivity.

The northernmost island group in Vanuatu, the **Torres Islands** contain the islands of Hiw (the largest and northernmost), Metoma, Tegua, Ngwel, Linua, Lo, and Toga. The archipelago is part of the Torba Province.

## Rivers

| River | Source | Mouth | Cities (if any) |
|---|---|---|---|
| **Sarakata (Espiritu Santo)** | Espiritu Santo | Pacific Ocean | N/A |
| **Lololima (Efate)** | Efate | Pacific Ocean | N/A |

## Lakes

The largest lake in Vanuatu, **Lake Letas** is situated in the center of Gaua Island in the Banks Islands in the northern part of the country. It surrounds Mount Gharat, the highest peak on the island, on three sides.

## Seas

Bordered by Australia, New Caledonia (France), Papua New Guinea, the Solomon Islands, and Vanuatu, the **Coral Sea** contains the world's largest reef system, the Great Barrier Reef (a UNESCO World Heritage Site). It is a popular tourist attraction for birds and aquatic life. It borders the Solomon Sea to the north, the Pacific Ocean to the east, Queensland to the west, the Tasman Sea to the south, and the Torres Strait (which connects it to the Arafura Sea) in the northwest.

## Economic Geography

**Currency** Vanuatu vatu

**Natural Resources** Fish

**Agricultural Products** Copra, coconuts, cocoa, coffee, kava, taro, yams, coconuts, fruits, vegetables, fish, beef

**Port** Port Vila

# Historical Geography

**Former Name** New Hebrides

**Historic City** Franceville (now Port Vila, est. 1889)

**Empires** British and French Empires (1906-1980)

**Natives** Melanesians

**Independence** From France and the United Kingdom, 1980

# Cultural Geography

**Language** Bislama, French, English (official)

**Major Ethnic Groups** Ni-Vanuatu (98.5%), other (1.5%)

**Religion** Presbyterian (32%), Roman Catholic (13%), Anglican (13%), Seventh-day Adventist (11%), other Christian (14%), John Frum Movement (5%), other (12%)

**Foods** Fish, taro, yams, papayas, pineapples, mangos, plantains, sweet potatoes

# Destinations

## Tourist Attractions

Having one of the few underwater post offices in the world, **Mele Island** offers many watersports to tourists. It is a small islet west of Efate, the site of Port Vila, the Ni-Vanuatu capital.

**Mount Yasur** (see Volcanoes)

Located in Mele Bay, a short ferry ride from Port Vila, **Iririki** is a popular tourist resort. The whole island is leased to the Iririki Island Resort.

The national cultural institution of Vanuatu, the **Vanuatu Cultural Center** is located in Port Vila. It aims to record and promote the traditional indigenous cultures of the country.

Located in the Vanuatu Cultural Center in Port Vila, the **National Museum of Vanuatu** specializes in exhibits relating to the culture and history of Vanuatu.

Located opposite Luganville, Vanuatu's second largest settlement, **Aore Island** is popular for diving and fishing. Large colonies of bats occupy the island's many caves.

## World Heritage Sites

On the islands of Efate, Lelepa, and Eretoka, the **Domain of Roy Mata**, a powerful 13th-century Melanesian chief, stretched over many of the islands of Vanuatu. According to legend, when Roy Mata conquered the land, his first goal was to unite the tribes. His elaborate grave is the main focus of the World Heritage Site, containing the bodies of over 25 members of his crew.

# sources

# sources

wikipedia.org

maps.google.com

# about the author

Born and raised in Irving, Texas (the thirteenth largest city in the state), **Pranay Varada** is a student at the School of Science and Engineering in Dallas. In May 2017, Varada was declared the champion of the 29th National Geographic Bee, the result of five years of hard work and dedication. Varada beat out 2.6 million competitors from around the country to win a $50,000 scholarship, a trip to the Galápagos Islands, and a lifetime membership to the National Geographic Society. Following his victory, Varada was presented with a proclamation from the City of Irving and a letter from Texas senator John Cornyn, and was given the opportunity to meet the Indian Prime Minister, Narendra Modi, in Washington, D.C.

Varada has been learning classical music since the age of four, and, in his free time, is an avid composer of music for the piano and other various instruments.

CPSIA information can be obtained
at www.ICGtesting.com
Printed in the USA
FSHW021953220721
83489FS